# Higher Returns from
# Safe Investments

# Higher Returns from Safe Investments

## Safe Investments

USING BONDS, STOCKS, AND OPTIONS TO
GENERATE LIFETIME INCOME

MARVIN APPEL

Vice President, Publisher: Tim Moore
Associate Publisher and Director of Marketing: Amy Neidlinger
Executive Editor: Jim Boyd
Editorial Assistant: Pamela Boland
Development Editor: Russ Hall
Operations Manager: Gina Kanouse
Senior Marketing Manager: Julie Phifer
Publicity Manager: Laura Czaja
Assistant Marketing Manager: Megan Colvin
Cover Designer: Chuti Prasertsith
Managing Editor: Kristy Hart
Project Editor: Betsy Harris
Copy Editor: Karen Annett
Proofreader: Williams Woods Publishing
Senior Indexer: Cheryl Lenser
Senior Compositor: Gloria Schurick
Manufacturing Buyer: Dan Uhrig

© 2010 by Pearson Education, Inc.
Publishing as FT Press
Upper Saddle River, New Jersey 07458

**This book is sold with the understanding that neither the author nor the publisher is engaged in rendering legal, accounting, or other professional services or advice by publishing this book. Each individual situation is unique. Thus, if legal or financial advice or other expert assistance is required in a specific situation, the services of a competent professional should be sought to ensure that the situation has been evaluated carefully and appropriately. The author and the publisher disclaim any liability, loss, or risk resulting directly or indirectly, from the use or application of any of the contents of this book.**

FT Press offers excellent discounts on this book when ordered in quantity for bulk purchases or special sales. For more information, please contact U.S. Corporate and Government Sales, 1-800-382-3419, corpsales@pearsontechgroup.com. For sales outside the U.S., please contact International Sales at international@pearson.com.

Company and product names mentioned herein are the trademarks or registered trademarks of their respective owners.

Printed in the United States of America

First Printing March 2010

ISBN-10: 0-13-700335-8
ISBN-13: 978-0-13-700335-8

Pearson Education LTD.
Pearson Education Australia PTY, Limited.
Pearson Education Singapore, Pte. Ltd.
Pearson Education North Asia, Ltd.
Pearson Education Canada, Ltd.
Pearson Educatión de Mexico, S.A. de C.V.
Pearson Education—Japan
Pearson Education Malaysia, Pte. Ltd.

Library of Congress Cataloging-in-Publication Data

Appel, Marvin.

   Higher returns from safe investments : using bonds, stocks and options to generate lifetime income / Marvin Appel.

      p. cm.

   Includes bibliographical references and index.

   ISBN 978-0-13-700335-8 (hbk. : alk. paper) 1. Investments. 2. Bonds. 3. Financial risk. 4. Retirement income—Planning. I. Title.

   HG4521.A657 2010

   332.63'2—dc22

                                   2009048198

*To my father Gerald Appel, with gratitude for his guidance and love all these years.*

# Contents at a Glance

# Contents

## Contents

# Acknowledgments

I extend my heartfelt thanks to Audrey Deifik, Joanne Quan Stein, Bonnie Gortler, and Lucas Janson for reading the drafts of this manuscript along the way. Their insightful feedback helped me stay on-message. I shudder to think how difficult it would have been to earn the editors' approval at FT Press without the benefit of their input in advance. I would also like to thank the staff at FT Press for bringing this book from my word processor into print so smoothly.

Lastly, I am grateful for the resources that were available on the Internet at no cost and which enabled me to do the research necessary to write this book. I have referenced all specific sources of information within the book, but I am particularly grateful to QuantumOnline.com, Moody's, Fitch Ratings, and the Chicago Board Options Exchange (CBOE).

# About the Author

**Marvin Appel** originally trained as an anesthesiologist at Harvard Medical School and Johns Hopkins Hospital. He concurrently earned a PhD in Biomedical Engineering from Harvard University. However, in 1996 he changed careers and joined his father in the field of investment management, where he has been able to put his engineering and computer training to work in analyzing the stock market. He is now CEO of Appel Asset Management in Great Neck, NY, which manages more than $45 million in client assets in mutual funds, exchange-traded funds, and individual stocks and bonds using active asset allocation strategies.

Dr. Appel's book *Investing with Exchange-Traded Funds Made Easy*, now in its second edition, was published by FT Press and was featured on CNBC's *Closing Bell* show. Dr. Appel and his father have also written *Beating the Market, Three Months at a Time*, published by FT Press and released in January 2008.

Dr. Appel is the editor of *Systems and Forecasts*, a highly regarded newsletter on technical analysis that his father, Gerald Appel, started in 1973. He is also a regular contributor to *Investment News*. Dr. Appel has been a regular contributor to *Dental Economics* and to *Physician's Money Digest*. His market insights have been featured on CNBC, CNNfn, CBS Marketwatch.com, and Forbes.com. He has been invited to testify to the New York State Legislature regarding his market forecasts and has presented his investment strategies to numerous conferences, including several chapters of the American Association of Individual Investors and, most recently, at the Canadian Society of Technical Analysts at their annual meeting in Toronto.

# chapter 1

# Introduction

> *"Give a person a fish and you have fed him for a day. Teach him to fish and you have fed him for life."*
>
> —*Chinese proverb (Lao Tzu)*

In the wake of the worst financial crisis since the Great Depression, many investors are wondering how they can get attractive returns while still being able to sleep at night. This book shows you how, using investments that generate income.

You might ask what this means. Isn't the goal of all investments to generate income? Actually, there are two ways you can profit in the financial markets. One way is to buy low and sell higher (hopefully), thereby generating *capital gains*. The allure of investing in search of capital gains is that when you are successful, the profits can be very large. The main disadvantage of investing for capital gains is the significant risk that you will lose money. Even if your investment is ultimately profitable, you do not know in advance how much you will make or when your profits will materialize.

The other way to profit, which is the subject of this book, is to own investments that pay you a stream of income in return for just holding them in your account, regardless of which direction the markets are moving. You can profit even during periods when the financial markets are flat. Bonds are a prime example of an income-generating investment: You buy a bond and collect the income every six months.

Dividend-paying stocks are another. Stocks generally pay quarterly dividends. Even if the stock goes up and down while you hold it, you will continue to receive the quarterly dividend check as long as the company continues to pay.

Let's take a minute to discuss why income investing could be good for you. The major advantage of income-producing investment strategies is their greater potential safety than those strategies that entail buying and selling in pursuit of profit. Another advantage of making an income-generating investment, especially in bonds, is that once you invest, you have a very good idea how much cash you will receive and when you will receive the payments.

So far, so good—as an income investor, you could possibly earn dependable income at reduced risk. What's not to like? The answer in today's markets is that many income-producing investments, including bank certificates of deposit, money market funds, and many bond investments, are simply not paying you as much as you need. One of the fundamental principles in investing is that you have to bear greater risk to earn higher returns. (Unfortunately, many investors have learned the hard way that simply bearing risk does not guarantee returns.) The implication would seem to be that if you invest for safety, you could be condemning yourself to modest, perhaps even inadequate, earnings. The goal of this book is to show you that this is not necessarily true. The pursuit of greater safety than you might find in the stock market or in real estate, for example, need not limit your returns to the meager rates now available from the average bond or bank CD.

Fortunately for the investor concerned about safety, as an income investor, you might not need to give up much, relative to what you might earn from riskier approaches. This book shows you that not all bonds are created equal, and that there are several areas of the bond market with above-average profit potential. Promising areas in 2010 include high-yield corporate bond funds and long-term individual municipal bonds. Because these types of bonds pay more than average, they also expose you to potential risks. You will learn how to mitigate those risks when we discuss each type of bond in more detail. Down the road, conventional bonds might again pay attractive levels of interest income. This book tells you what you need to know to become an informed investor in such bonds, whether through mutual funds or with a brokerage account in which you buy bonds from individual borrowers.

You will also learn about two types of stock market investments that have been less risky than the overall stock market and which can be good sources of ongoing income: stocks with above-average dividends and a strategy using exchange-traded funds and stock options known as **covered call writing**. Moreover, in the right amounts, these stock market strategies can improve your returns (compared with holding only bonds) with very modest amounts of added risk.

The income-generating strategies you will learn from this book are those that have been safer than the typical investment in the stock market and have the potential to return more than the average investment in the bond market. Although the future performance of any investment strategy cannot be predicted or guaranteed, you will see how much risk has been associated with different income investments and you will learn how to manage that risk in the future. Even without a guarantee, you should be able to sleep at night.

# How Much Money Do You Need to Retire?

Yogi Berra once said, "If you don't know where you are going, you might end up someplace else."[1] In the context of retirement planning, you should interpret Berra's wisdom to mean that you should not retire until you have established and achieved a prudent set of financial goals.

As a general rule, I counsel clients to *plan on spending up to 5% of their retirement savings each year if they don't want to deplete their savings over time.* Although no future results can be guaranteed for any investment program, the assumption behind this advice is that it should be possible to earn an average of 5% per year on your investments without taking unacceptable levels of risk. To the extent you earn more than 5%, you should save any surplus to help keep up with inflation and to provide a cushion for those years when your earnings fail to meet your expenses. If you can limit your expenses to 5% or less of your savings each year, your savings might last you indefinitely. On the other hand, the greater the amount you withdraw from your savings to spend each year, the greater the chances that you will deplete your investments and possibly run out of money.

Let's see how this works with an example. Suppose you have saved $250,000 in your 401(k) plan; 5% of that amount is $12,500, which is the amount you should be able to safely withdraw from your 401(k) plan each year to spend. Now, I realize that very few retirees are living on $12,500/year. Fortunately, you will also receive Social Security and, if you are lucky, perhaps a pension from your job. Your retirement budget should be within the sum of all these sources of income: 5% of your retirement savings plus Social Security plus any other pensions.

Another example in reverse: Suppose you decide that after taking Social Security and other pension income into account, you still want to be able to withdraw $50,000/year from your investments. How much do you need before you retire? You would divide $50,000 by 5% (which is 0.05) to get the answer, in this case $1 million. If you want to be able to spend $50,000/year from your investments without taking on too much investment risk, you need to have saved $1 million.

According to the longevity tables that the IRS uses to calculate required minimum IRA distributions (IRS Publication 590 at www.irs.gov), a couple that retires when both spouses are 65 will, on average, need to support one or both spouses for another 26 years. A lot of crazy things can happen in 26 years: inflation, recession, economic dislocations, and more. You don't want to find yourself short of money in your seventies if events take an unexpected turn. Rather, you need to be confident that the money you had when you retired will still be there in 10 or 15 years. Achieving that confidence requires investing with both safety and returns in mind, and limiting the rate at which you spend your money to a sustainable level of 5% or less of principal each year.

## Let's Get Started...

The next two chapters describe what you need to know about bonds, including how they work, how you can invest in them, and what their risks are. Following that, the book shows you various strategies for investing in the safest types of bonds. To increase your potential returns, I recommend including some less-conservative income strategies in your portfolio: high-yield bond mutual funds, preferred stocks, and stock market strategies (high-dividend exchange-traded funds and covered call writing). Such strategies are the subject of Chapters 7, 9, 10, 11, and 12. The final chapter shows you how much of your capital to allocate to the different strategies described in the book. There is no single correct answer—the best investment program for you depends on how much income you need, how long you expect to need it, and how much risk you are willing to accept. Chapter 13 presents some choices for your consideration. Ultimately, the goal of this book is to show you how to invest safely for attractive returns that could potentially sustain you for years to come.

# chapter 2

# Basics of Bond Investments

If you are planning for retirement, you want to be able to sleep well at night without having to worry about whether your investments will pay you enough to live on. A thoughtful program of investing in bonds can help you achieve this peace of mind. This chapter explains what bonds are, how they work, and why they are usually (but not always) safe. This chapter covers several different types of bonds. Some offer absolute safety but relatively low returns, whereas others offer very high-potential returns but with significant risk. Some or all of these bonds have a role in your investment program.

## What Is a Bond?

A bond is a loan that an investor makes to a business or government. Bond investors make loans, and in return receive regular interest payments. You might be familiar with loans from your own borrowing. For example, if you have a mortgage, you make an interest payment each month and, in addition, pay down a bit of the principal so that by the time the mortgage ends, everything is paid off. Bonds are a little different—they resemble interest-only mortgages. A company borrows $1,000 from you and during the life of the loan pays you only the interest due. When the bond (loan) matures, you get the principal back as a lump sum.

If you were deciding to borrow money, you would naturally evaluate whether the amount of interest charged is reasonable and whether you will be able to pay back the loan on the date it is due. As a lender, you also have to evaluate both of these factors, this time from the other side of the table.

The bond market uses a special name to describe the interest rate on the loan that you, the investor, are extending: the **coupon rate** (also called **coupon yield**). This originated because in the past, bonds were physical pieces of paper that included attached coupons that specified the amount and date of each interest payment due during the life of the bond. Bond investors would turn in the coupons for each scheduled payment and collect the cash due. In the United States, bond interest payments generally occur every six months.

Bonds are usually sold in units of $1,000. (That is, whoever owns bonds at maturity will receive $1,000 for each bond.) So, a bond that pays $50/year in interest is said to have a coupon rate of 5% because $50 represents 5% of the original and final principal of $1,000 per bond. The amount for which a bond will be redeemed when it matures (usually $1,000) is called its **par value**.

Short-term bonds are those that mature in three years or less. Long-term bonds mature in more than ten years. Bonds that mature in three to ten years are intermediate-term bonds. Most of the time, short- and intermediate-term bonds will be the suitable maturities for you because they offer the best balance between the level of investment risk and return, as you will see later in this chapter. I generally do not recommend long-term bonds to individual investors except in special situations.

# Why Bonds Are Safe

From the moment you buy a bond, you know when you will receive scheduled interest payments and how much they will be. You also know the date at which you will get your principal back. In contrast, when you buy a risky investment like a stock, you do not know what

*bias is showing*

your returns will be or how much you will end up with at any future point in time.

If you buy a bond and plan to hold it until it matures, the only way it can disappoint you is if the borrower fails to live up to his end of the bargain by failing to make a scheduled payment of interest or principal. That is called a default, and occurs rarely. You will see how to recognize bonds with low default risk—the ones that are truly safe investments.

*= b safer not truly safe.*

# How Much Money Have Bond Investors Made in the Past?

The answer to this question depends on the type of bond you are talking about. This section reviews the long-term history for four important broad categories of bonds: three-month Treasury bills, Treasury bonds, corporate bonds, and municipal bonds.

Three-month Treasury bills (T-bills) are virtually free of risk. They represent borrowing from the U.S. Treasury that will be repaid in three months. The federal government can literally print money to pay off its debts, so there is no default risk. And since the term of these bonds is so short, price fluctuations during the three months you hold a T-bill are negligible. You are guaranteed to receive the full par value of the T-bill just by sitting tight for three months.

The Treasury borrows significant amounts of money for longer periods, up to 30 years.[1] As with T-bills, there is no default risk in any of the Treasury debt included in this index. However, the prices of existing Treasury bonds do fluctuate as interest rates change (see the section on interest rate risk later in the chapter). Indeed, there have been periods when a portfolio of Treasury bonds would have lost money such as 1994, 1999, and 2009.

9

Corporate bonds are debt issued by businesses. Unlike the federal government, businesses can neither print money nor compel anyone to buy from them, so there is always a risk that a business will not be able to pay off its bondholders. When a business fails to pay the interest or principal due to bondholders, that business is said to default. In that case, bondholders usually suffer a significant investment loss. Corporate bonds default infrequently unless they are already flagged by public analysts' reports as having elevated credit risks. (Chapter 3, "Risks of Bond Investing," discusses credit risk in more detail.) However, because corporate bonds do expose investors to the risk that the borrowers might default, they have to pay higher interest to attract investors than does the federal government.

Municipal bonds represent borrowing by state and local governments or other government entities. The advantage of municipal bonds compared with Treasury or corporate bonds is that municipal bond interest is mostly exempt from federal and state income taxes. Municipal bonds have earned a reputation for safety as well as for their tax advantages because state and local governments have rarely defaulted on their debt obligations. However, if you look back to the 1970s, you can see that this type of bond too has had its periods of significant risks. With many state and local governments facing revenue shortfalls in 2010, you should not take the safety of municipal bonds for granted. Look for more details about this in Chapter 8, "Municipal Bonds—Keep the Taxman at Bay."

Table 2–1 shows the average compounded annual gain from different types of bonds during the 36-year period 1/1/1973–12/31/2008.[2] Also listed in the table is the largest investment loss (as a percentage) from a peak to a subsequent low point in the value of portfolios of these different bonds, which is called the drawdown. **Drawdown** is a measure of risk that will be more fully discussed in Chapter 3. For the purposes of interpreting Table 2–1, the closer to zero a drawdown, the safer the investment, and the more negative a drawdown, the riskier the investment.

Table 2–1  *Gains and Investment Risk for Different Types of Bonds, 1973–2008*

| Type of Bond | Compounded Annual Investment Gain 1973–2008 (%) | Worst Peak-to-Valley Drawdown (%) |
| --- | --- | --- |
| Three-month Treasury bills | 6.6% *reasonable* | 0% |
| Barclays Capital U.S. Treasury Index | 8.4% | -7.4% |
| Barclays Capital U.S. Credit Index (corporate bonds) | 8.1% | -19.3% |
| Municipal bond fund average[3] | 5.6% | -22% |

*least volatile.*

# For Bonds, Past Is Not Prologue

If future bond returns were guaranteed to be as high as the historical results in Table 2–1, you would be set for life with little risk. Unfortunately, as of early 2010, bond market conditions indicate that returns will be far lower for the foreseeable future.

The most important factor that determines how much you will make from bonds is the current level of interest rates. When prevailing interest rates are high, bond investors will earn good returns. When prevailing interest rates are low, bond investors will earn less. Because interest rates in late 2009 were low by historical standards, bond investors had to search hard for ways to make attractive returns without assuming too much risk. This will likely remain the case at least through 2010. Table 2–2 compares the average level of interest rates from 1973 to 2008 with rates in late 2009.[4] You should not get the impression from Table 2–2 that interest rates from 1973 to 2008

11

spent a lot of time near the average values reported here. The 1973–2008 period encompassed an extremely wide range of interest rates. However, for most of this period, bond yields were higher than they are now. Figure 2–1 shows the yield available from ten-year Treasury notes from 1973 to 2009 as an example of how widely interest rates have varied and how low they have fallen by historical standards.

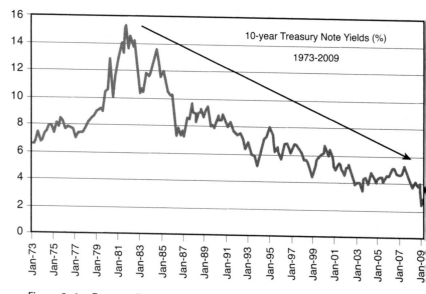

**Figure 2–1**   *Ten-year Treasury note yields, 1973–2009*

Notice that corporate and long-term municipal bond yields are not too far below historical precedent, but Treasury yields are far lower now than they were in 1973–2008. This means that bond investors today are looking at better return prospects from buying corporate or municipal bonds than from buying Treasury debt *provided that they can address the question of the added risk.*

Table 2–2   *Interest Rates in 2009 Compared with Historical Averages*

| Type of Bond | Average Yield 1973–2008 | Market Yield, November 2009 |
|---|---|---|
| Three-month Treasury bill | 5.9% | 0.02% |
| Treasury bonds | 7.0% | 1.8% |
| Corporate bonds | 9% | 5.7% |
| Long-term tax-exempt bonds[5] | 6.6% | 4.4% |

You can also see from Table 2–1 that the historical risk from buying corporate or municipal bonds has been very large at times. (The 19.3% loss in the value of corporate bonds occurred in 1979–1980, when rising interest rates and a recession dealt a double whammy to the corporate bond market. The 22% loss in the average national municipal bond fund occurred from 1979 to 1981. We will see in later chapters why these developments hurt bonds back then, why they might conspire to do so again in the future, and what you can do to protect yourself.)

# Which Type of Bond Is Right for You?

Bonds share the basic characteristic of providing you with a dependable source of investment income. However, there are many different types of bonds from which you can choose. Let's see how you can best meet different requirements with the various bonds available to you.

## Taxable Versus Tax-Exempt

The interest you earn from a bond is subject to different rates of taxation, depending on who issued it. You will pay the heaviest taxes on interest that you receive from bonds issued by for-profit corporations. Interest on such a bond is subject to federal and state income taxes at the highest rate your income level incurs. (Unlike dividends on stocks held for more than six months, there is no tax reduction afforded to investors who collect bond interest.)

The federal government issues Treasury bonds. What the feds give, they take back (partially) by imposing federal income taxes on the interest you earn. However, Treasury bonds are not taxable at the state or local level.

The interest on bonds issued by state or local governments is not taxed at all *if held by a resident of the issuing state.* Such state or local government bonds are also referred to as municipal bonds or tax-exempt bonds. Note that if you live in New York and you buy a Connecticut municipal bond, you will have to pay New York State income taxes but not federal income tax. On the other hand, if you as a New Yorker buy a New York tax-exempt bond, you save both federal and state income taxes. In this way, high-tax states such as New York or California give significant incentives to their residents to buy bonds from in state.

Because tax-exempt bond interest escapes taxation, state and local governments do not have to pay as much interest as taxable corporations to attract investors. If you are in a high tax bracket, the amount of bond interest you get to keep after taxes will likely be higher for a tax-exempt bond than for a taxable corporate bond of similar risk and maturity. On the other hand, if you are in a low tax bracket, municipal bonds might be less remunerative than taxable bonds. You have to evaluate the impact of taxes for yourself in deciding which bond pays the better after-tax yield. If you are buying bonds for an IRA or similarly tax-deferred account, you should, of course, buy taxable bonds.

Let's see how you can compare a taxable bond with a tax-exempt bond. For example, suppose that federal and state income taxes claim 35% of your taxable bond interest. If you have a taxable corporate bond that pays 6% per year, after you pay taxes you will be left with 3.9% per year. Any municipal bond that pays more than 3.9% per year will, therefore, be more profitable for you. If tax rates rise so that your tax bracket climbs to 40%, a municipal bond paying just 3.6% will match the interest income you receive from a 6% taxable bond.

There is an important caveat regarding the extent to which municipal bonds are truly tax-exempt. First, interest on some tax-exempt bonds (called **private activity bonds**) is subject to the alternative minimum tax (AMT). This means that if you are already paying AMT or fear that you might, be sure that any municipal bond you purchase is exempt from AMT as well as from regular income taxes. (Most municipal bonds are exempt from AMT.)

## SOCIAL SECURITY RECIPIENTS BEWARE

There are situations where receiving "tax-exempt" interest can increase your tax bill. For example, the more income you earn, the more of your Social Security benefits will be subject to federal income tax. For the purposes of deciding how much income tax you have to pay on your Social Security benefits, even tax-exempt bond interest counts as income. If the receipt of tax-exempt interest increases your tax bill, is that interest really tax-exempt? (No.) So, if you are receiving Social Security and less than 85% of your Social Security benefits are taxable, the comparison between the true after-tax yield from a taxable or tax-exempt bond can be complicated. The worksheet for calculating the extent to which your Social Security benefits are taxable can be found in IRS Publication 915. (Enter "publication 915" in the search window on the IRS home page at www.irs.gov.)

## Investment Grade Versus High Yield

The majority of corporate and tax-exempt bonds that are issued are called *investment grade*, which means that they have a low risk of failing to deliver on the promised payments of interest and principal. In contrast, high-yield bonds (also called junk bonds) are those that independent ratings agencies judge to have significant risks of failing to pay up. As a result of the perceived risks, high-yield bonds have to pay greater levels of interest to attract investors.

In later chapters, you learn about credit ratings and about how to manage your investments in high-yield bonds (specifically, in high-yield bond mutual funds). Here, Table 2–3 provides a brief overview to compare investment-grade versus high-yield bonds.

**Table 2–3** *Comparison of Investment-Grade and High-Yield (Junk) Bonds*

| Feature | Investment-Grade Bond | High-Yield Bond |
| --- | --- | --- |
| Risk of loss | Usually low | Potentially high |
| Level of interest income | Low | High |
| Predictability of returns | High | Low |
| Best way to invest | Individual bonds or mutual funds | Mutual funds mandatory |
| Level of ongoing oversight required of you | Low | High |

# Interest Rate Risk

Suppose you bought a ten-year bond last year (that is, the bond matures ten years after it was issued). Now you read that interest rates are going up. Does this mean that the interest you receive from your bond investment will go up too, and if not, what happens to your bond?

The important point to understand, and a point that confuses many investors, is that regardless of what happens to interest rates, once you buy a bond, the level of interest income is locked in for the remaining life of that bond, regardless of what happens to interest rates. The borrower can no more change the rate of interest they are paying you than you can decide to change the amount you pay on a fixed-rate mortgage. That is why bonds are considered safe. Likewise, the $1,000 per bond that you receive at maturity will not change, regardless of what happens to interest rates. The only way that the expected interest income or return of your bond principal can decrease is if the borrower defaults. We examine the issue of defaults later on; in 2008–2009, borrower default became a significant problem for bond investors.

But if the interest and principal you receive from a bond never changes, what does it mean to say that interest rates have changed? The answer is that changes in interest rates reflect the cost of *new* borrowing, but do not represent changes in the terms of preexisting loans. If you bought a bond that pays 5% per year and interest rates rise to 6% per year, the borrower who sold you your bond would have to pay a higher rate to attract new investors. That would naturally be a disappointment. If you had known interest rates were going to rise, you could have held out for better terms. Conversely, if interest rates fall, you continue to receive the old, higher rate and can take satisfaction in the prescient timing of your investment.

The risks that bond investors face from changes in interest rates are twofold: opportunity risk and price risk. You have already seen an example of opportunity risk. If you buy a bond before interest rates go up, you have lost the chance to get higher returns down the road from the money you already committed. However, if you determine that the income from a 5% bond is sufficient to meet your needs, you don't really need to worry if interest rates rise as long as you hold your bond until maturity.

Price risk is another matter. That occurs only when you want to buy or sell a bond at some point between the time it was issued at $1,000 per bond and its maturity, when it will be redeemed at $1,000 per bond. The issue of price risk is of crucial importance to investors who purchase bond mutual funds, so we discuss it in more depth here.

17

Suppose you buy a bond for $1,000 that pays $50/year in interest ($25 every six months) and that matures in ten years. That is a 5% bond. After you buy the 5% bond, interest rates rise to 6%, which means that each newly issued $1,000 bond will pay $60/year in interest for ten years. Now suppose that an emergency arises and you cannot wait for your 5% bond to mature, and instead decide to sell it on what is called the secondary market (the bond market equivalent of eBay). What will your bond be worth?

An investor who buys your old bond will get only $50/year, whereas a new bond would pay $60/year per $1,000 invested. Therefore, no investor in her right mind would pay you $1,000 to get just $50/year. You will have to sell your bond at a loss.

But, you might object, whoever buys your bond will get the full $1,000 at maturity in ten years. Shouldn't that count for something? Indeed it does. An investor has a choice: She could buy your bond that pays just $50/year for less than $1,000, both receiving interest and making a profit at maturity when she gets $1,000 from the bond she bought from you for less. Or she could buy a new bond for $1,000, collect $60/year, and get back her $1,000 at maturity (no profit there).

The market price of your bond will be the price where the person who buys it from you would be neither better off nor worse off buying from you than buying a newly issued bond with the same maturity date from the same issuer. *The take-home point is that there are two sources of investment returns from a bond: the interest you receive during the life of the bond and the difference between the price you pay for a bond and the $1,000 per bond you get when it matures.*

Returning to the situation when interest rates change: Suppose you bought a 5% bond (i.e., it pays $50/year in interest) for $1,000 and interest rates subsequently drop to 4% per year. Newly issued bonds, therefore, pay only $40/year. If you wanted to sell your 5% bond in the secondary market, you would sell for more than $1,000—the drop in interest rates earned you a profit. The fair price for your bond would be the price where the value of the higher interest payment ($50/year from your bond versus $40/year from new bonds) is offset by the loss in value between now, when your old bond is worth more than $1,000, to maturity when it will be worth exactly $1,000.

To summarize: When interest rates rise, the market value of existing bonds falls. When interest rates fall, the market value of existing bonds rises. If you hold individual bonds to maturity, changes in interest rates will not affect the returns you receive from your investment.

# How Much Is Your Bond Really Paying You?

In the preceding section, we saw that if you buy a bond at some point between the time it was issued and the time it matures, you might pay a price different from $1,000 per bond—sometimes significantly different. Remember: All bonds are issued in units of $1,000. If interest rates rose from the time the bond was issued, its market price will be under $1,000. If interest rates fell since issuance, the market price of the bond will exceed $1,000.

If you buy a bond at less than $1,000, which is called **below par** (par value being exactly $1,000), and hold it until maturity, you receive two sources of profit. The first source is the interest payments. The second source is the profit accrued when the bond you bought for less than $1,000 is redeemed at maturity for $1,000.

Conversely, if you pay more than $1,000 for a bond, which is called **above par**, you will receive interest during the time you own the bond, but at maturity you will lose money when you receive just $1,000 per bond.

The amount you earn from holding a bond results from the combination of these two events: coupon payments while you hold the bond and the difference between what you paid for the bond and the $1,000 it is worth at maturity. The overall investment return that takes both of these events into account is called the **total return**.

## YIELD-TO-MATURITY: VERY IMPORTANT

Let's look at a specific example. Suppose you pay $904 for a bond that pays $45/year in interest and that matures in ten years from the time of your purchase. First, note that the original coupon rate (also called coupon yield) was 4.5% because $45/year is 4.5% of the $1,000 issue price. However, because you bought the bond at a discount (that is, below its par value of $1,000), the interest income as a percentage of your purchase price is $45/904 = 5.0%. (Annual interest income as a percentage of the current market price of a bond is called the **current yield**.)

In addition, your initial outlay of $904 will be worth $1,000 in ten years. The growth of a $904 investment to $1,000 in ten years represents a compound rate of return of 1.0% per year, which is in addition to the 5.0% per year interest. As a result, your total return will be 6.0% per year, which is the annual interest plus the annual price appreciation assuming you hold until maturity. This amount of 6.0% per year is called the **yield to maturity**. The yield to maturity is the most important piece of information you need to know about a bond when evaluating whether or not you find the returns attractive.

Suppose you have the choice of buying a ten-year bond with a 6% coupon yield for $1,000 or the bond in the preceding example. Which would be the more profitable investment? The answer is that the returns are the same. It is the yield-to-maturity that allows you to compare the future returns from one bond with another. When you go to your broker and ask for the selection of available bonds, you will see the coupon yield and also the yield to maturity. The yield to maturity is more important.

*I cannot overemphasize the importance of the distinction between the coupon yield and the yield to maturity.* In a time when interest rates are very low (as they were in 2008 and 2009), most Treasury and many corporate bonds sell above par and have coupons that exceed current interest rates. Do not be blinded by the temptation of a "4% bond" in an era of 2% interest rates: You will most likely be paying above par, so that your total return will be 2% per year, not 4% per year.

# Why Long-Term Bonds Are Riskier Than Short-Term Bonds

Interest rate changes do not affect the prices of all bonds by the same amount. The prices of bonds maturing soon, called *short-term* bonds, do not fluctuate much, whereas the prices of *long-term* bonds can be very volatile when interest rates change.

To see why this is the case, consider a bond that will mature in one week. If interest rates are 5.2%, each $1,000 bond earns $1/week in interest.[6] (5.2% of $1,000 is $52/year in interest, which is $1/week.) Suppose interest rates double to 10.4% (which would be a cataclysmic event in the bond market). Then new bonds would pay $104/year, or $2/week. The change in interest income is just $1 per $1,000 bond over its remaining one-week life, which means that the price change should be correspondingly small.

If you think that interest rates are going to rise, you should invest in short-term bonds. That way, if rates rise, your bonds will not lose much value and, when they mature, you will soon have the opportunity to reinvest at higher rates. The ultimate short-term bond fund is a money market fund, whose share price is expected (but not guaranteed) to stay at $1 regardless of what happens to interest rates.

At the other extreme, consider a 30-year bond. If you buy a 30-year bond paying 5% and, subsequently, interest rates rise to 6%, you are stuck with a below-market level of coupon interest for a very long time. A 1% rise in interest rates will take a big toll on the value of such a bond. Figure 2–2 shows an example of how a 1% change in interest rates up or down affects the price of a short-term (2-year), intermediate-term (7-year), and long-term (20-year) bond when each started at $1,000 with a coupon of 5%. As expected, the same move in interest rates will cause a much bigger change in the price of a long-term bond than in the price of a short-term bond.

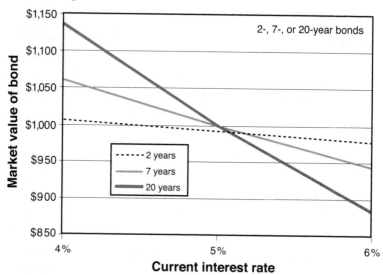

**Figure 2–2**   *How a change in interest rates affects the values of bonds with different maturities*

The fact that long-term bonds have greater price risk is one reason why, most of the time, long-term bonds pay higher interest rates than short-term bonds. As a bond investor, you face a trade-off. If you stay invested only in short-term bonds, your investments will be safe from changes in interest rates, but your returns will be lower compared with the investor who bore the interest rate risk of longer-term bonds.

Most of the time, the best balance between interest rate risk and reward (in the form of interest income) for individual investors is with intermediate-term bonds maturing in seven to ten years, *assuming that you are confident that the issuer of your bonds will be around that long.* Unfortunately, during 2009–2010, investors cannot neglect the risk of issuer bankruptcy, particularly in high-risk industries such as financial services. That argues for buying corporate bonds that mature in one or two years in any potentially vulnerable company.

## BOND DURATION VERSUS BOND MATURITY

You might come across the concept of *duration* in addition to maturity, especially if you investigate bond mutual funds (which we discuss in Chapter 5, "Bond Mutual Funds—Where the Best Places Are for Your One-Stop Shopping"). Unfortunately, this can create some confusion. Even though both are expressed in years, duration and maturity are not the same. *Duration is a measure of how much the value of a bond or bond portfolio changes when interest rates change by a fixed amount:*

%change in bond price $\approx$ -change in interest rate $\times$ bond duration

(The negative sign is in the formula because a rise in interest rates causes a fall in bond price.) For example, if interest rates rise 0.2% from 5% to 5.2%, the value of a bond with a duration of five years will fall by approximately 1%.

Because longer-term bond prices are more sensitive to changes in interest rates than shorter-term bond prices, the duration of a longer-term bond is higher than the duration of a shorter-term bond, all else being equal. For any bond that pays coupon interest, the duration is less than its maturity. You could use Microsoft Excel, for example, to calculate the duration of the hypothetical bonds in Figure 2–2 when interest rates and their coupon rates are both 5%: The 2-year bond has a duration of 1.92, the 7-year bond has a duration of 6.0, and the 20-year bond has a duration of 12.9. Figure 2–2 shows that a change of 1% in interest rates up or down did indeed produce a change of about 6% in the price of the 7-year bond, and the price changes in the other bonds in Figure 2–2 were likewise proportional to their durations.

Duration is not constant for a bond. It changes when interest rates change. A decline in interest rates from 5% to 4% would change the duration of the 20-year bond slightly, from 12.9 to 13.3 years, whereas the duration changes in the shorter-term bonds would be negligible. Of course, changes in interest rates do not affect the maturity of a bond.

If you are mathematically inclined, there is an excellent, concise derivation of duration online at www.regentschoolpress.com/BondDuration.pdf.

# How to Buy Individual Bonds

If you want to buy a bond, you need to go to a broker. Most of the well-known stockbrokers (Schwab, T.D. Ameritrade, and so on) can sell you individual bonds. To buy bonds, you first need to open an account at a broker and deposit sufficient funds to pay for the investments you plan to make.

Once the account is open and funded, you can go shopping. Retail brokerages usually display the list of available bonds on their Web site. You can peruse the available selection. If you see the same bond offered on a broker's Web site for different prices, it means that there is more than one firm trying to sell the same bonds.

In addition to the coupon yield, maturity date, and price, you can also get the credit rating on available bonds from most brokers' Web sites. Credit ratings are one analyst's opinion as to the relative likelihood that a bond will pay the promised interest and return of principal. You can refer to Chapter 3 to find out more about credit ratings.

Several things about buying bonds are not readily apparent on review of brokers' Web sites. First, unlike stocks, there is usually no specified commission per trade for buying bonds. Rather, buying bonds more closely resembles buying a car. The price you pay includes a profit for the dealer.

Like buying a car, and unlike buying a stock, you can sometimes negotiate a better price for a bond than what is posted on the broker's Web site. One of my favorite tactics when buying individual bonds for my own account (when it was at Smith Barney) was to ask if the firm had any odd lots that they wanted to get rid of. Odd lots are bond holdings below $10,000 (that is, fewer than 10 bonds). Such odd lots can be great investments for individual investors to hold to maturity, but for large bond dealers,[7] they are an annoyance and financially insignificant. As a result, dealers might sell odd lots to you for a better-than-normal price just to simplify their bookkeeping.

Conversely, if you go to a broker looking only to buy an odd lot of a particular bond of which the dealer has plenty of inventory, you might have to pay significantly more than if you were shopping for a round lot of at least $10,000. Only by asking will you know if a dealer is willing to sell to you for a lower price than originally asked, or if he is bumping up his price to sell you an odd lot.

Another way in which buying and selling bonds resembles dealing with a used car is your experience when you want to sell back to the dealer. You will frequently find when you go to sell a bond from your account before it matures that the price you are offered is much less than you think the bond is worth. Indeed, the price offered to you might be well below the value stated for your bond on your brokerage statement, just as the value a car dealer offers for your trade-in is frequently far below the Kelley Blue Book price.

There is not much you can do about lowball offers for your bonds except to ask your broker to post them for sale at the price you want and hope that someone takes you up. As a general rule of thumb, you can expect to lose 2% of your investment if you try to sell your individual bonds on the open market before they mature. (Treasury debt is easier to sell than bonds from other types of issuers.) For this reason, you should buy only those individual bonds that you are confident you can hold until maturity. If getting your money back on short notice is important to you, you should consider bond mutual funds, discussed in Chapter 5.

# Understanding Bond Listings

Table 2–4 shows an example of the type of information you are likely to find on a broker's Web site when you look for bonds to buy. (This information is a corporate bond listing from T.D. Ameritrade's Web site on 4/22/09.) This section discusses each of the pieces of information that have not already been covered.

Table 2–4  *Bond Information*

| CUSIP # | Credit Ratings | Quantity | Issuer | Coupon | Maturity Date | Yield (to Maturity) | Price |
|---------|---------------|----------|--------|--------|---------------|---------------------|-------|
| 427866-AN-8 | A2/A | 50 | Hershey Co. | 5.2% | 9/1/2011 | 2.014% | 107.485 |

- **CUSIP number**—A unique nine-character identification for each publicly traded stock and bond
- **Credit ratings**—An assessment from one or more different rating agencies about how risky this bond is (see Chapter 3)

- **Quantity**—The number of bonds available at the listed price
- **Issuer**—The company or government entity who is doing the borrowing
- **Coupon**—The percentage of $1,000 principal paid out each year in interest
- **Maturity date**—The date when the bondholders get their principal back
- **Yield to maturity**—The actual investment return you will get if you buy the bond at the quoted price and hold it until maturity
- **Price**—A dollar amount quoted in units of $10, so a price quote of "100" means $1,000, and the price quote of 107.485 in this example means $1,074.85 per bond

# Buying Bonds Far from Coupon Payment Dates

Recall that bonds pay interest only twice per year, on dates specified at the time the bond is issued. Suppose a bond makes its semiannual coupon payments on January 15 and July 15, and you are shopping for bonds on January 14. At first glance, you might see the opportunity to receive six months' interest in just one day by purchasing a bond the day before the scheduled coupon payment.

Of course, if something seems too good to be true, then it is. When you buy a bond, you pay not only the price of the bond but also a pro rata share of the coupon payment you will receive. For example, if a bond pays $20 every six months and you buy it three months before the next coupon payment, you will pay the seller for those three months' interest, in this case $10 per bond. If you buy a bond the day before the coupon payment, you will have to pay the seller for the entire coupon amount less one day's interest.

As a general rule, when you hold bonds in a brokerage account, the value of those bonds that the broker reports to you on your statement will not include the accrued interest, which is the interest earned since the last coupon payment that has not yet been paid to you.

# Conclusion

This chapter made a number of points, hopefully allowing you to judge whether bond investments are suitable for you:

- Individual bonds are safe investments with predictable returns.

- Interest rates are lower now than they have been in past decades, particularly for Treasury issues.

- There are different kinds of bonds with different levels of credit risk, ranging from Treasuries that cannot default to junk bonds that frequently default, especially during recessions. You learn how to deal with a wide range of bond investments later in the book.

- Short-term bonds yield less than long-term bonds (most of the time).

- When interest rates change, the market value of outstanding bonds also changes. Rising interest rates go along with falling bond prices, while falling interest rates go along with rising bond prices. The longer the maturity of the bond, the more its price changes in response to a change in interest rates.

- Shopping for individual bonds can be like shopping for a car: The astute comparison shopper is usually rewarded with a better deal.

# chapter 3

# Risks of Bond Investing

Because the goal of this book is to help you earn the best returns consistent with a reasonable degree of safety, it is important to know what level of returns you might achieve with different types of bond investments. Although the public considers bonds to be safe—and for the most part this reputation has been justified—in 2008 and early 2009, some areas of the bond markets experienced unprecedented losses. Your goal is to avoid the potential minefield that is today's bond market. This section explains what you have to watch out for.

## How to Measure Risk—Drawdown

Drawdown is a visually intuitive way to measure risk. A **drawdown** is the percentage loss from a high point to a subsequent low point in the value of an investment. This is most easily understood with a visual example.

Figure 3–1 shows some recent history (December 2008–May 2009) of the iShares Barclays 20+ Year Treasury Index Fund (TLT), which represents all Treasury bonds maturing in 20 years or longer. (This fund is actually an exchange-traded fund, or ETF. ETFs behave like mutual funds but you buy and sell them the same way you would buy or sell shares of stock.) During the six months shown, the highest value of this investment was $120.53, on 12/30/2008. The subsequent lowest value of the investment during this period was $94.71. Because $94.71 is 21% less than $120.53, the drawdown during this period was 21%. Figure 3–1 indicates how you would calculate the drawdown by measuring data off of the graph. You can perform a similar visual analysis or calculation if you use Internet resources such as Yahoo! Finance to chart the value of investments, locate the peaks and valleys, and calculate the percentage difference from each peak to each subsequent valley.

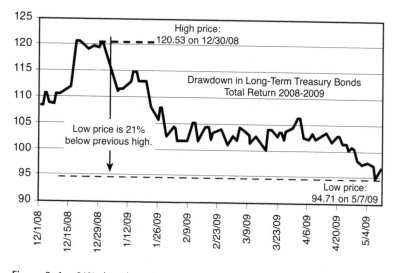

**Figure 3–1** *21% drawdown in long-term Treasuries, 2008–2009*

As a general rule, long-term bond prices are very volatile and, therefore, can be expected to experience recurring significant drawdowns. Figure 3–2, which contains the total return of the iShares 20+ Year Treasury ETF (TLT) from 2002 to 2009, illustrates this point. The 21% drawdown shown in Figure 3–1 was the worst to hit long-term Treasuries since 2002, but there have been other significant losses as well that are circled in Figure 3–2.

The nice thing about using drawdown as a measure of risk is that it reflects the actual pain you would have experienced if you had been in the investment during the period of loss. Other measures of risk that you might see reported (beta, standard deviation) are not as directly related to your experience as an individual investor. When you work with drawdown as a risk measure, you need to keep a few points in mind.

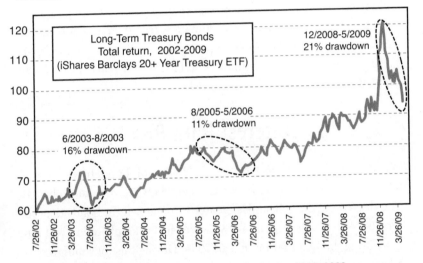

**Figure 3–2**  *Selected drawdowns in long-term Treasuries, 2002–2009*

First, if your measurement of past risk is going to be helpful to you, it is important to look at data that includes sufficient market history. Consider what the financial markets have done from 2000 to 2009. In October 2002, the stock market experienced a major low; after this low, stocks and high-yield bond funds, among other risky investments, made big gains for five years, until late 2007. If you were evaluating the risks of a proposed investment in late 2007 and you looked back only five years, you would have gotten an unrealistically rosy view of your potential risk and returns.

For better or worse, 2007–2009 showed us an unusually high degree of market risk in a variety of different investments. If you include these years in your future risk analyses, you will probably not be lulled into a false sense of security regarding the potential risks of any investment.

Second, with bond investments, interest income represents the majority of the investment gains you will achieve. This means that it would be best for you to take interest income into account when measuring historical drawdowns, especially if you are examining periods longer than half a year. Unfortunately, free data available online frequently omits the favorable impact of interest income on the performance of bond mutual funds or ETFs, which could lead you to overestimate the level of historical risk.

# Interest Rate Risk

We already discussed in Chapter 2, "Basics of Bond Investments," that the prices of existing bonds change when interest rates change. The degree of price change is greater for longer-term bonds than for shorter-term bonds. Figure 3–3 shows a vivid example of interest rate risk during the first four months of 2009. During this four-month period, Treasury bonds lost money because interest rates rose. As would be expected, there was very little price movement in short-term Treasuries (1–3 Year Treasury Index). At the other end of the spectrum, long-term Treasuries (20+ Year Treasury Index) lost fully 18% as the yield on 20-year Treasuries climbed from 3% per year to 4% per year. If you were unfortunate enough to buy long-term Treasuries at the start of 2009, you would have lost six years' worth of interest income in just four months. Of course, if interest rates had fallen instead of rising, you would have made money just as quickly.

The take-home message is that you should not buy long-term bonds unless you are certain that you will be satisfied with the level of interest income because if rates rise after you invest, you will be down a lot of money. As a general rule, bonds that mature in longer than ten years expose you to price risk that is excessive compared with the added increment in yield with bonds that mature in seven to ten years.

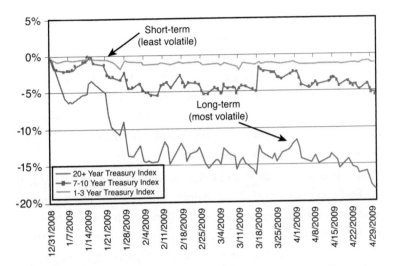

**Figure 3–3**  *Total returns of short-, intermediate-, and long-term Treasuries, 12/31/08–4/30/09*

# Default Risk

The worst thing that can happen to your bond portfolio is for one (or more) of the bond issuers to default. **Default** means that a bond fails to pay a scheduled interest or principal payment. It is basically equivalent to bankruptcy. Once a bond defaults, the trustees of a bond issue negotiate with the borrower and other creditors to salvage what they can of the bondholders' original investments.

You might think that when a bond defaults, your investment is wiped out. Fortunately, things are not quite that bad: The average defaulted bond has historically returned 40 cents on the dollar, although that amount can be highly variable.[1] In the recessionary climate of 2009, defaulted bonds are expected to pay far less than normal—perhaps just 20 cents on the dollar, on average.

33

No matter how you slice it, defaults are catastrophic for your investments. As a safety-conscious investor, you should avoid bonds that you believe have any significant chance of defaulting. Steps that I, as an investment manager, take to reduce credit risk include checking a bond's credit rating and the outlook for any change in credit rating, as well as checking to see if the company is earning enough to easily cover the burden of its interest payments and reviewing other analysts' outlook on the company's stock.

When it comes to the risk of defaults, there is good news and bad news. The good news is that, on average, the risk of defaults by any investment-grade bond is normally so low that you do not need to worry about it if you are well diversified. The bad news is that 2009–2010 is not a normal time, with the risk of default higher than normal.

If default risk is your sole concern, U.S. Treasury debt is the most direct solution. The government can literally print all the money it needs to pay off its debt, so there is no risk of default. This absolute guarantee is the reason why foreign central banks have invested so much in U.S. Treasury debt and Agency Debt (such as bonds issued by Fannie Mae and Freddie Mac). The downside is that Treasury debt pays less interest than other types of bonds.

# Credit Ratings

Because default would be a disaster financially, how can you avoid the risk? If you have the time, temperament, and training, you could examine publicly filed financial statements from a bond issuer to see if the borrower had sufficient assets and profits to cover its current debt obligations. That would still not guarantee your future safety because a company's condition can change, but it would, at least, be a good start. In fact, information readily available on MSN Investor or Yahoo! Finance allows you to do just that.

Fortunately, if you are not a do-it-yourself credit analyst, bond issuers offer you another option. To attract investors, most bond issuers pay a ratings agency (a private company) to perform a financial analysis and to report on its findings. There are two major credit ratings agencies in the United States: Moody's and Standard & Poors. A third company that is less well known but whose perspectives I often find useful is Fitch Ratings.

As a bond investor, you are effectively a subscriber to these agencies' research (whether you realize it or not) when you note a bond's credit rating. A credit rating is just a letter grade that encapsulates the relative creditworthiness of a bond. Table 3–1 summarizes the credit rating scale used by the big agencies and the historical implications of credit rating on the likelihood of default.

There are some important lessons to be drawn from Table 3–1. First, even though a listing of different credit ratings from highest to lowest (i.e., AAA, AA, A, BBB, etc. in the Standard & Poors rating scale) gives the feeling of a steady progression of risk, in fact the risk of default mushrooms as credit ratings get lower down the scale. If you buy a long-term, BBB-rated bond, the risk of default over the life of that bond is significantly higher than the risk of a long-term, A-rated bond. (Table 3–1 lists 5-year default risks, but if you look out further than that, to 20 years for example, the BBB bond looks increasingly dangerous compared with the higher investment-grade rankings.)

Table 3–1 does not list the gradations within each category, but when you evaluate an individual bond, you might see a Moody's rating of Baa3. That is below Baa2, which, in turn, is below Baa1, which is below A3, etc. In the Standard & Poors/Fitch Ratings scale, each letter rating might be modified by a "+" or "-," so that a BBB+ bond has a higher rating than a BBB bond, which, in turn, is higher than a BBB- bond. When you are dealing with the universe of Baa-rated bonds, those gradations can represent significantly different levels of risk. In fact, you should be very wary regarding Baa3 (analogously, BBB-) bonds because during times of trouble, they have defaulted significantly more often than Baa2 or Baa1 (analogously, BBB or BBB+).

Table 3–1    *Historical Default Rates for Corporate Bonds with Different Credit Ratings*

| Moody's Rating | Standard & Poors or Fitch Ratings | Percentage of Outstanding U.S. Corporate Bonds as of 12/31/2008[2] | Average 5-Year Default Rate, 1920–1999[3] | Worst Historical 5-Year Default Rate for Bonds Issued 1970–1999[4] |
|---|---|---|---|---|
| Aaa | AAA | Investment grade, 6% of U.S. bonds | 0.2% | 2.1% |
| Aa | AA | Investment grade, 17% of U.S. bonds | 1% | 1.8% |
| A | A | Investment grade, 36% of U.S. bonds | 1.4% | 1.9% |
| Baa | BBB | Investment grade, 24% of U.S. bonds | 3.5% | 5.3% |
| Ba and below | BB and below | Junk bonds (17% of U.S. corporate bond market) | 16% | 33% |

Although credit ratings are very helpful, there are a number of reasons why this simple letter grade does not totally protect you against default risk. First, companies' financial conditions can change rapidly. For example, Lehman Brothers (an investment bank) enjoyed an "A" credit rating right up until the time of its bankruptcy in September 2008. The value of its assets in derivatives suddenly evaporated when those derivatives' values were updated to reflect market conditions. Enron also enjoyed a high credit rating until almost the end, although in this case the rating was the result of outright fraud by Enron executives.

Second, the implications of a good (or bad) credit rating depend in large part on the economic environment. In 2007, for example, fewer than 1% of junk bonds defaulted; however, in 2002, 16% of junk bonds defaulted because the economy was much weaker in 2002. As we will see later in the section "Credit Downgrade Risk," credit ratings are updated periodically and might decrease as the result of a deteriorating business climate. But as a practical matter, ratings do not quite keep up with changes in the business climate, so during a recession, a bond with a given credit rating will be riskier than that same-rated bond during a strong economy.

Third, just as a grade of A in a basket weaving class does not imply the same level of intellectual achievement as an A grade in an advanced physics class, so too the same credit rating has had very different implications for different types of bonds. For example, as of 12/31/2008, the industry with the lowest proportion of junk bonds was the financial industry,[5] despite the fact that many large firms (that are also large debtors) failed in 2008 or were kept alive only through extraordinary government bailout measures. Indeed, as of mid-2009, many financial company bonds with good credit ratings were selling as cheaply as junk bonds, indicating that the bond market is taking these companies' solid credit ratings with a grain of salt.

Another even more glaring example was the rampant grade inflation in mortgage-backed bonds. Whereas only 2% of outstanding corporate bond debt was rated AAA at the end of 2007, fully 60% of "structured products" were. (Structured products in the bond market consisted mainly of bonds backed by pools of mortgages, as distinct from a loan to a bondholder to an individual corporate borrower.) Many of these structured products turned out to be very risky and lost a large part of their original value.[6]

Despite these caveats, an effective way of addressing the problem of default risk is to stay with very short-term corporate bonds—those maturing in two years or less. Even though we have seen examples of companies that collapsed suddenly, it is far more common that companies that defaulted did so only after several years of deteriorating credit ratings. If you buy very short-term bonds, historical precedent suggests that it is very unlikely that a bond that carried an investment-grade rating when you bought it would end up defaulting within two years.

## Credit Downgrade Risk

If a borrower runs into trouble (as frequently occurred in 2008 and 2009), credit-rating agencies can reduce the credit rating of outstanding bonds if they determine that a company has become less secure. When that happens, the price of outstanding bonds usually drops (all else being equal). The only case when a drop in credit rating does not depress the price of bonds is when the bond market has already anticipated the downgrade. This means that between the time you buy a bond and the time you are paid back at maturity, you bear credit risk.

If you hold a bond to maturity and it does not default, your return over the life of your investment will be what you expected when you bought the bond regardless of what happens to its credit rating. Nonetheless, you do not want to buy bonds that you fear might be downgraded, first because you want to sleep at night, and second, because if you thought a bond was going to be downgraded, you would wait for that to occur and buy the bond after the downgrade had occurred, presumably at a lower price (higher yield).

In 2008 and 2009, it became clear that the bond market has a mind of its own in setting the price of individual corporate bonds, regardless of the credit rating. For example, many financial companies such as Bank of America enjoyed high (AA) credit ratings in early 2009 even as the prices of their bonds fell, anticipating troubles ahead. Credit ratings are most useful in comparing companies within similar industries, but during difficult times should not be relied upon as the only safety measure.

# Inflation

Inflation is the biggest risk to the bond investor (except for inflation-indexed bonds). When you buy a bond, your future profits are fixed. However, thanks to inflation, your income needs will rise during the period of time you hold your bonds. The challenge is to put together an investment program where your returns will be high enough to meet your current needs *and* to increase over time to help you keep up with inflation. Unless you have saved far more than most, it is impossible to meet both of these goals over a term of 20 years or more with only individual bonds.

If you hold a long-term bond that pays 6% per year interest at a time when inflation is running only 3% per year, you might feel in good shape. However, if inflation should jump to 8% per year, you are in trouble: You have locked in a rate of return guaranteed to lose purchasing power even if you don't spend a dime on yourself. 8% inflation is not unthinkable. During the 1970s, inflation averaged 7.4% per year, and during the first half of 2008, consumer prices rose at an annualized rate of 8% per year. As of early 2010, inflation remains under control, but the federal government policies of running large budget deficits and of "quantitative easing" (i.e., printing money) could be very potent stimulators of future inflation once the recession eases.

Generally speaking, interest rates move in the same broad direction as inflation. During periods of rising inflation (for example, 1966–1979), interest rates rose. During periods of falling inflation (for example, 1982–2003), interest rates fell. If you are concerned about rising inflation in the years ahead (as you should be in 2010), you should favor short-term bonds (five years or less to maturity) over long-term bonds (more than ten years to maturity). If inflation does rise in the years to come, you will probably be able to reinvest your short-term bond holdings at higher rates when they mature, which will help protect the purchasing power of your investments in the event that inflation does spike.

## DIGRESSION ON INFLATION HEDGING

Which investment has been the best hedge against inflation? Gold comes to mind, but there is an even more precise hedge that would historically have done a good job of preserving the purchasing power of your money. Gold has actually been a leveraged bet that inflation will rise: The price of the metal has increased strongly during periods of rising inflation and decreased during periods of falling inflation. That is not the same as saying that if you put your savings into gold, the value of your investment would have kept up with prices. If inflation rises from 2% per year to 4% per year, gold will probably perform well. However, if inflation falls from 5% per year to 3% per year, gold investors will probably lose money even though prices are rising all the while.

No—the best inflation hedge has been *Treasury bills.* If you had kept all of your money in three-month Treasury bills (in a tax-deferred account), you would have lost very little ground to inflation even during the worst of times.[7]

Suppose you have saved up 20 years' expenses, and you and your spouse are both over 80 years old. In that case, you might plan to deplete 5% of your principal each year without taking too great a risk of running out of money. In this situation, placing all of your investments in Treasury bills would be a viable option. Each year you could withdraw what you need to spend, while remaining confident that your remaining investments would increase at approximately the same rate as your cost of living.

There are many caveats here. First, expenses are not uniform. Rather, large exigencies arise from time to time, and you would have to plan your budget to allow for such emergencies. Second, many retirees want to leave money behind for their heirs, in which case the all-Treasury bill portfolio would be a poor choice.

# Liquidity Risk

If you need your money back before a bond matures, you will have to sell your bond on the open market. As we have already mentioned, this implies that you will take a loss (or will forfeit some prior gains) on your investment. But just how much it will cost you to sell before maturity varies, depending on market conditions. If many panicky investors are selling the same type of bond at the same time, you will take a bigger hit by selling with the herd than if you were selling the same bond under more normal market conditions. This means that if you sell a bond in response to unexpected bad news about the issuer, your losses can be very large—potentially reaching 5%–10% of the par value.

To minimize your exposure to liquidity risk, you should keep some of your capital in cash or in bond mutual funds so that you never have to sell an individual bond urgently. Chapters 5, "Bond Mutual Funds—Where the Best Places Are for Your One-Stop Shopping," and 8, "Municipal Bonds—Keep the Taxman at Bay," recommend some bond funds that should be safe and rewarding repositories for your money.

# Market Catastrophes—The Example of Asset-Backed Bonds

The 2007–2009 period saw many unexpected and unprecedented losses in the financial markets. Let's look at one example that serves as a warning: If one of your investments starts to show losses well beyond what historical precedent would lead you to expect, you should cut your losses and liquidate.

One previously strong bond investment that soured is floating rate funds. These are mutual funds that invest in bank loans with adjustable interest rates. For several years (2003–2006), these funds appeared very attractive. The yields were good, and there was no interest rate risk because if rates were to rise, the yield on the funds' holdings would also rise. As a result, unlike most of the rest of the bond market, a rise in interest rates would not normally cause the price of the fund to decline.

Also, the loans in these mutual funds were often backed with specific collateral. In contrast, most bonds are backed by the borrower generally, but not by specific collateral that the bond issuer had to pledge as a condition of selling bonds to the public. Historically, bank loans backed by collateral have lost less in the event of default than have unsecured bonds. These two advantages combined to produce steady returns at virtually no risk—until mid-2007.

At that point, investors began to question whether bank loans were really worth what the banks said they were and, specifically, whether the collateral backing them was actually worth as much as the loan balances. Investors began to shun bank loans, making them impossible to sell except at very reduced prices. Figure 3–4 shows the total return of one of the better-established floating rate funds, the Oppenheimer Senior Floating Rate Fund (XOSAX). From the start of October 1999 until July 2007, the fund returned an average of 6% per year with extremely little risk. Even during the 2001–2002 period, which was difficult for corporate and high-yield bonds, the fund held up well. However, starting in July 2007, Oppenheimer Floating Rate became more volatile than it had ever been, and started to slip. It really fell off a cliff in September 2008, ultimately hitting bottom at the end of 2008, 31% below where the fund stood at the end of June 2007.

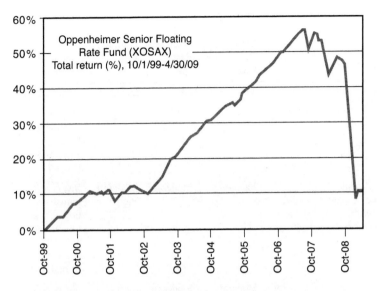

**Figure 3–4** *Total return of the Oppenheimer Senior Floating Rate Fund, 1999–2009*

# Conclusion

This chapter has discussed several sources of risk if you decide to invest in bonds. Table 3–2 summarizes the relative danger that each of these risks poses to you for each type of bond. The only way to completely avoid risk is to invest all of your capital in Treasury bills. However, at their current yield near zero, Treasury bills will not generate the returns you need to support yourself over the long term. Rather, your strategy should be to invest in a number of different types of bond investments so that your exposure to any one type of risk is limited.

Table 3–2  *Overview of Risks for Different Types of Bonds*

| Type of Bond | Default Risk | Credit Downgrade Risk | Interest Rate Risk | Liquidity Risk | Risk Management Strategy |
|---|---|---|---|---|---|
| Treasury bills | None | None | Low | Low | None needed |
| Long-term Treasury | None | None | High | Low | Stay with intermediate-term Treasuries instead |
| Investment-grade corporate (intermediate term) | Low | Moderate | Moderate | Moderate-High | Diversify industries; buy only as much as you are certain you can hold to maturity |
| Tax-exempt investment grade (intermediate term) | Low (for general obligation bonds) | Moderate | Moderate | High | Diversify by geographic area; buy only as much as you are certain you can hold to maturity |
| High-yield bonds (junk bonds) | High | High | Moderate | High | Only invest in high-yield bonds using mutual funds, and use a stop-loss strategy (see Chapter 7, "High-Yield Bond Funds—Earn the Best Yields Available while Managing the Risks") |

# chapter 4

# Bond Ladders—Higher Interest Income with Less Risk

The bond investor faces a conundrum. On the one hand, interest rates are at historically low levels even though there is a glut of government bonds for sale and inflation looms as a threat. These considerations would argue in favor of investing in short-term bonds. On the other hand, you can get higher rates of interest if you buy long-term bonds. This is especially true for the municipal bond investor. If your tastes run toward Treasury bonds (because you cannot tolerate any credit risk), the spreads between short- and long-term bonds are also very wide.

If you are undecided about whether to assume the risks of long-term bonds to garner their higher interest payments or whether to settle for currently meager short-term rates, the strategy of bond laddering that you will learn about in this chapter might help. Bond laddering requires some effort to get the program started, but after that, you will not have much work to do.

## How a Bond Ladder Works

A bond ladder is just a portfolio of individual bonds whose maturity dates are (more or less) evenly spread from short term to longer term. For example, you could have a portfolio where 20% of the bonds mature in two years, 20% in four years, 20% in six years, 20% in eight years, and 20% in ten years.

Setting up a laddered portfolio in this way is easy enough conceptually, but the real benefit of the bond-ladder strategy arises not when you set up the portfolio, but rather after years of reinvesting principal from maturing bonds into long-term bonds. You will see why this is useful in the following example.

Suppose that one-year bonds pay 1% interest per year, two-year bonds pay 2% interest per year, and three-year bonds pay 3% interest per year. (This is an unrealistically wide spread between different maturities that is used just for illustration.)

If you buy $10,000 in each of these three maturities, you will invest $30,000 total. For the purposes of this example, let's assume that you started in 2010 and, therefore, bought bonds maturing in 2011, 2012, and 2013. Once you set up your portfolio, your interest income will be 1% of $10,000 (one-year bonds) plus 2% of $10,000 (two-year bonds) plus 3% of $10,000 (three-year bonds), for a total of $600. The average yield on your portfolio is $600/$30,000 which is 2% per year. (It is not a coincidence that the average maturity in your portfolio is two years, and the yield of the portfolio is what you would earn from a portfolio that consisted entirely of two-year bonds. In the real world, it does not always work out exactly this way, but is usually close.)

After one year, in 2011, $10,000 of the one-year bonds will mature. You should reinvest this $10,000 in three-year bonds that mature in 2014. Let's assume that interest rates have not changed, so that three-year bonds still pay 3% per year. After you do so, your portfolio will consist of the following:

- $10,000 in bonds that mature in 2014 and pay 3% (most recent purchase, these bonds mature in three years)

- $10,000 in bonds that mature in 2012 and pay 2% (two-year bonds purchased in 2010 that have one year left until they mature)

- $10,000 in bonds that mature in 2013 and pay 3% (three-year bonds purchased in 2010 that have two years left until they mature)

After another year passes, in 2012, $10,000 of the original two-year bonds that you purchased in 2010 will mature. You should reinvest in three-year bonds. If interest rates remain the same, your portfolio will consist of the following:

- $10,000 in bonds that mature in 2015 and pay 3% (most recent purchase, these bonds mature in three years)

- $10,000 in bonds that mature in 2014 and pay 3% (three-year bonds purchased in 2011, these bonds now have just two years left until they mature)

- $10,000 in bonds that mature in 2013 and pay 3% (three-year bonds purchased in 2010 that now have just one year left until they mature)

Table 4–1 summarizes these events. Look at where your portfolio will stand in 2012. Every bond in the portfolio will be paying 3% per year because by 2012 every bond was purchased with a maturity of three years. But you won't have to wait three years to get some principal back. Instead, you will get one third of your principal back every year, and the average maturity of your portfolio is just two years and not three. In effect, you are getting *coupon interest* commensurate with three-year bonds from a portfolio whose average maturity is just two years.

Suppose that instead of using bonds from one to three years maturity, you assemble a more typical bond ladder with maturities of two, four, six, eight, and ten years. In that case, every two years one fifth of your bonds would mature and you would reinvest that amount in ten-year bonds. After four such reinvestments (eight years), every bond in your portfolio will pay coupon interest characteristic of ten-year bonds even though the average maturity of your portfolio will be just six years. From then on, you would continue the process of reinvesting every cohort of maturing bonds in ten-year bonds to maintain the laddered portfolio.

Table 4–1    *Evolution of a Bond Ladder*

| Start in 2010 | In 2011 | In 2012 |
|---|---|---|
| $10,000 matures in 2011 (one year), paying 1% coupon | $10,000 matures now; reinvest this in bonds maturing in 2014 (three years) that pay 3% coupon | $10,000 matures now; reinvest this in bonds maturing in 2015 (three years) that pay 3% |
| $10,000 matures in 2012 (two years), paying 2% coupon | $10,000 matures in 2012 (one year), paying 2% coupon | $10,000 matures in 2014 (two years), paying 3% coupon |
| $10,000 matures in 2013 (three years), paying 3% coupon | $10,000 matures in 2013 (two years), paying 3% coupon | $10,000 matures in 2013 (one year), paying 3% coupon |

We have just seen that bond laddering has the potential to increase the level of coupon interest you receive, but how does this help you with interest rate risk? Suppose that rates rise, which would normally reduce the value of your bond portfolio. Your existing bonds will indeed fall in price before their maturity dates, but each year as a cohort matures, you will receive the full par value and you will be able to reinvest the proceeds at the higher interest rate that is then in effect. Of course, if rates fall, you will have to reinvest each cohort of maturing bonds at lower rates.

The overall effect of bond laddering on interest rate risk is that the interest rates at which you buy your bonds will end up being an average of available rates over the years—sometimes at high rates and sometimes at low rates. At a time like 2009–2010 when interest rates are at the low end of their historical ranges, bond laddering makes a lot of sense because you will reap the coupon interest from long-term bonds without bearing their full interest rate risk.

Bond laddering works on individual bonds, which can be of any type (investment-grade corporate, conventional Treasury debt, Treasury Inflation-Protected Securities, agency, municipal). You can also ladder target-date bond mutual funds in which every bond in the fund's portfolio matures in the same year. An example of such funds is the American Century Target Funds, which mature in 2015, 2020, or 2025. These American Century funds hold what are called zero-coupon Treasury bonds that mature in the year specified for each fund. There is no credit risk, but there is a lot of potential price volatility between now and the maturity date of these funds' portfolios. If Treasury yields become more attractive (i.e., more than 4% per year on the ten-year Treasury note), these funds might be attractive possibilities for the investor concerned about credit risk.[1]

Normally, you would not ladder bonds ranging from one to three years as in the illustrative example. Ideally, you should start bond laddering years in advance of when you want to start living off of your investments. For example, if you start your bond ladder ten years in advance and your longest bond is ten years, then by the time you reach year ten, all of your bonds will be paying coupon interest commensurate with ten-year bonds.

If you start far enough in advance, you don't even have to buy bonds of each maturity all at once. You could, for example, buy $10,000 in ten-year bonds every year for the next ten years. By the start of the tenth year, you will have a $100,000 laddered portfolio in which every bond pays coupon interest commensurate with ten-year bonds.

# Conclusion

Bond laddering is a safe strategy that is suitable for you if you have a brokerage account in which you can buy individual bonds. Constructing a bond ladder portfolio for yourself will ultimately generate the high levels of coupon interest that characterize long-term bonds without tying up all of your assets in such bonds. Bond laddering removes the necessity of having to time the bond market because your bond ladder will ultimately represent the average of interest rates available.

# chapter 5

# Bond Mutual Funds— Where the Best Places Are for Your One-Stop Shopping

You might like the idea of bonds—an investment with predictable returns that are likely to exceed inflation with low risk. But you might be overwhelmed by the hundreds of different individual bonds available to you, or you might not have a broker you trust, or you might not have enough money to buy a diversified portfolio of individual bonds. Don't despair—bond mutual funds can come to your rescue. By investing in a low-cost bond index fund recommended in this chapter, you can outperform the majority of bond investors. This chapter provides a small number of other recommendations for you as well. But even if you want to expand your horizons and seek out bond mutual funds on your own, you only need to know a few things, which are covered in this chapter.

## Bond Mutual Funds Can Reduce Your Transaction Costs

Mutual funds allow individual investors access to literally hundreds of different bonds with a single purchase. The bond mutual fund pools investments from all of its shareholders, and invests that big pool of money for them. Each shareholder owns, indirectly, a proportional slice of the entire portfolio. Moreover, mutual funds allow individual investors to hire professional management at (usually) reasonable prices. Most mutual funds require a typical minimum investment in the $3,000 range and have thousands of shareholders and, therefore, millions of dollars under management.

You have already seen that the minimum investment in individual bonds is $1,000 and, as a practical matter, is many times that. Individuals who buy single bonds from a broker are likely to get overcharged because brokers and dealers price bonds so that each transaction generates a minimum amount of revenue for the firm. To get a reasonable price, you typically need to buy at least five to ten bonds ($5,000–$10,000) at a time. Mutual funds almost always purchase large enough blocks to get attractive prices.

Not only do mutual funds allow you indirectly to purchase bonds at good-customer prices, they also allow you to cash out of your bond investment at no cost. Remember, when you try to sell your bonds back to a dealer, you can expect to receive several percent less than the market value reported on your brokerage account statement. However, if you sell your mutual fund shares, you get the same price as a buyer would pay on the same day. Moreover, you don't have to worry about being penalized for transacting with only a small amount of money because the price per share you pay or receive when you buy or sell a mutual fund is the same regardless of the size of the transaction.

# Bond Mutual Funds Reduce Your Risk through Diversification

It is natural to worry about investing too much of your money with any one borrower, just in case they go bankrupt, which would prevent them from paying you the promised interest and principal. (The federal government is an exception, as already mentioned.) The solution is to buy bonds from many different issuers, which is called **diversification**. For example, in my money management practice, I do not invest more than 1%–2% of a client's capital in the bonds of any one business, just in case.

But as an individual, if you want to buy bonds from at least ten issuers and, wanting to pay a fair price, have to buy $10,000 in each, you have to have $100,000 to invest in bonds. If you have only $10,000 to invest in bonds altogether, a bond mutual fund is probably a better choice. In this chapter, I suggest some of the most attractive bond mutual funds that should be worthy of your trust.

# Expenses in Bond Funds

The services of a bond fund manager and the administrative support he or she requires come at a price. That price is called the **expense ratio** of the mutual fund, and represents the amount the fund management takes each year from the shareholders' investments as pay for services rendered. The expense ratio is charged against the total assets in the fund, not just the profits.

For example, most bond funds have an expense ratio of about 1% per year, which means that if the bond investments in a fund earned 5% last year, the fund management took 1%, which left 4% profit for the shareholders. The expense ratio is a cost in addition to the transaction costs that the fund pays when it buys or sells bonds from its broker—the way you would do individually, but on a much larger scale.

There is no way to avoid paying a fund's expense ratio. However, all else being equal, a lower-expense mutual fund will be more profitable for you than a higher-expense one. In the current era of low interest rates (the average investment-grade bond is paying less than 4%), it is hard for a fund manager to add enough value to overcome a 1% expense ratio. Vanguard is known for having rock-bottom expenses in many of its bond funds, typically under 1/4% per year.

# Sales Charges (Loads) in Bond Funds

Every mutual fund has an expense ratio, but many funds impose the additional, separate cost of a sales commission. Unlike the expense ratio, you can (and must) avoid paying sales charges, which are also called sales loads. These can amount to several percent of your investment.

Some brokers charge the sales load of several percent up front, so, for example, if you were to invest $10,000 in a fund, the initial value of your investment would be only $9,650 if the sales load is 3.5% (that is, the broker takes 3.5% of your $10,000 outlay—$350—leaving only $9,650 to work for you). This can occur when you buy "class A" shares from a commission broker like Morgan Stanley, Smith Barney, or Merrill Lynch.

More insidious are the "class B" shares, where there is no up-front sales charge but an additional 3/4% is taken out of your investment each year and paid to the broker. This is in addition to the fund's expense ratio. Suppose you unwittingly buy a class B share and later learn your return is being reduced by 3/4% per year compared with what you would be getting if you had purchased the same fund at a discount broker. Naturally, you would try to sell your class B shares and move to the more remunerative investment at your discount broker. Too bad. When you buy a class B share, you are locked in for up to seven years. If you try to exit before your term is up, the broker takes the unpaid sales charge as a lump sum called a back-end sales charge.

The only way you should buy bond funds is either directly from a no-load fund company such as Vanguard, or through a discount broker (for example, Schwab, T.D. Ameritrade) where there is a large selection of funds you can buy without paying a sales load. (As a registered investment advisor, I can buy class A shares in many mutual funds for my clients through discount brokers without their having to pay the up-front sales charge, in addition to the assortment of no-load funds.) When it comes to buying mutual funds, look before you leap: Make sure that there are no sales loads, up-front sales charges, or back-end sales charges.

# Other Expenses

Some funds charge you a penalty if you do not hold onto them long enough. For example, one of my favorite conservative bond funds is FPA New Income (FPNIX). It charges you 2% if you sell your shares within 90 days. The Vanguard High Yield Corporate Bond Fund (VWEHX) charges you 1% if you sell in less than a year.

These redemption charges are not the same as back-end sales charges because if you pay them, they go into the fund for the benefit of the other shareholders. Early redemption fees do not compensate salespeople. Nonetheless, you do not want to pay redemption fees. Either invest in funds that do not impose them (most do not), or invest only as much as you are certain you can leave in place for the required amount of time.

Lastly, if you buy a mutual fund through a discount broker, you might have to pay a transaction charge. Transaction costs at discount brokers can vary widely, depending on the particular fund, the size of your account, and the amount you are purchasing. Some discount brokers allow you to buy from a list of funds with no transaction cost. You should comparison shop to find the discount broker with the lowest transaction charges and the widest selection of funds available to you at no transaction costs.

# The Biggest Drawback to Bond Mutual Funds—No Maturity Date

We have already seen that when you buy an individual bond and hold it until maturity, you know from the day you make that purchase what your investment returns will be during the life of the bond (unless there is a default). With bond mutual funds, that is not the case.

Bond funds continually receive interest and principal payments. The fund manager quickly reinvests these cash flows so that all of the fund's assets are working for the shareholders virtually all the time. However, this means that the fund's portfolio is a moving target with no single maturity date. You can never ride out the bond market's fluctuations confident that at some point all of your investment will be returned to you, and when you buy a bond mutual fund, you cannot know what your future returns will be the way you can when you buy individual bonds (assuming none of your bonds defaults). The only mutual funds that are exceptions to this rule are certain target-date funds (such as the American Century funds mentioned in Chapter 4, "Bond Ladders—Higher Interest Income with Less Risk") designed to invest in bonds that mature at the same time.

# It Can Be Difficult to Know How Much Interest Your Bond Fund Is Paying

Probably the most difficult thing about researching bond mutual funds is finding out how much interest the bonds in their portfolios are paying. Recall that when you buy individual bonds, the piece of information of overriding importance in understanding the future return from your bond is the *yield to maturity*. If you have a portfolio of bonds, you can calculate its overall yield to maturity by averaging the yields to maturity for each of the component bonds.

For reasons I do not understand, many bond funds are opaque about the overall yield to maturity net of fees that they offer their shareholders. As a result, when you look on publicly available resources to secure this information, you might be misled.

## Pitfall #1—Current Yield or Distribution Yield

Suppose you have a bond fund whose share price is $10 and which is paying interest distributions at a rate of 50 cents per year. If interest rates remain rock stable, what will your return be from holding this fund for a year? If your answer is "I don't know," then you are correct.

The 50 cents/year represents coupon payments from the bonds in the fund's portfolio. In this example, the *distribution yield* of the mutual fund is 5% because the annual distributions equal 5% of the fund's share price. However, these distributions do not take into account whether or not the bonds in the portfolio are trading at a premium over par or at a discount. If the average price of the bonds in this fund's portfolio happens to be 100 (i.e., at par), then the *distribution yield* is a good measure of your expected total return if interest rates remain constant. (The **current yield** is the amount of coupon interest that the fund receives at an annual rate divided by the value of the fund's holdings. Before making a distribution, the mutual fund deducts its expenses, so the **distribution yield** of a fund's portfolio is the current yield of its portfolio minus expenses.)

However, interest rates in early 2010 are at long-term lows, so most outstanding bonds are trading above par now and will lose value as they approach maturity. The process of bond prices moving from a current market value away from par ($1,000/bond) to par value as they approach maturity is called the **pull to par**. The fact that the average investment-grade bond now trades above par means that the share prices of most bond mutual funds will decline over the coming years even if interest rates remain stable. Of course, if rates rise, share price losses will be even greater.

As a general rule, bond mutual fund distributions do not take into account how the pull to par changes bond prices as they approach maturity. As an individual taxpayer, you have the *option* of adjusting your annual interest income from taxable bonds to reflect the pull to par,[1] but mutual funds do not do this. Instead, mutual funds must realize the gains or losses from the bonds they buy in the year in which those bonds mature or are sold. *In the early 2010 environment of low interest rates, the current yield or distribution yield is likely to overstate the actual return of your bond fund.*

### Pitfall #2—Yield to Maturity

The yield to maturity of your fund's portfolio is what you need to know, but there is one additional wrinkle when dealing with a mutual fund that does not arise when you are evaluating individual bonds: mutual fund expenses. If you go to a fund's Web site and find the yield to maturity of the fund's portfolio of bonds, that return does not account for fund expenses. You have to locate the "expense ratio" of the fund (usually available on the same Web site as the yield to maturity) and subtract that expense ratio yourself.

# The Gold Standard—SEC Yield

If your fund reports an SEC yield, that is the single most informative piece of data to describe the potential return from the fund if interest rates and credit ratings remain stable. The **SEC yield** is the yield to maturity less the fund's expenses.

Here is an example of how important it is to get the correct yield when evaluating a bond fund. Suppose you were enticed by the performance of the Goldman Sachs Short Duration Government Fund (GSTGX) from 9/30/08 to 3/31/09, a period in which it returned more than most other short-term Treasury funds. If you wanted to look further into the fund, you might check Yahoo! Finance (http://finance.yahoo.com), where you would find the reported yield for the Goldman Sachs fund to be 3.36% per year. This is too good to be believed: At a time when ten-year Treasury notes were paying less than 3.2% per year, here a lower-risk, short-term bond fund was ostensibly paying 3.36%.

If you looked at the historical dividend distributions, you would note that as of 4/30/09, the fund (GSTGX) was distributing 2.53 cents per month on average during the first quarter of 2009, which worked out to an annualized distribution yield of 2.8% per year—not as good as the yield that Yahoo! Finance reported but still attractive compared with other Treasury investments. The only way to resolve the discrepancy is to find out the SEC yield, which you could accomplish with a visit to the Goldman Sachs fund's Web site.[2] The Web site revealed that as of 3/31/2009, the SEC yield was indeed 2.8%.

There are literally thousands of investment-grade bond mutual funds available to you, but only a small fraction of these are worthy of your attention. This chapter lists a handful of bond funds that have had superior long-term performance characteristics: either above-average returns or below-average risks, or both. Although nobody can guarantee the future performance of any investment, I would be surprised if using the bond mutual funds described here did not place you in better stead than the vast majority of bond fund investors. I do not claim that this is an exhaustive list of the best bond funds, and would be happy to hear from you if you have other suggestions.

# The Hurdle Bond Funds Have to Clear: Barclays Capital U.S. Aggregate Bond Index

The ideal benchmark against which to measure the performance of the bond funds you select is the most broadly diversified index of the

59

U.S. investment-grade bond market: the Barclays Capital U.S. Aggregate Bond Index.[3] This index goes back to 1976 and includes taxable bonds maturing in at least one year from three main areas of the U.S. bond market: Treasury bonds (34%), mortgage-backed bonds (43%), and corporate bonds (23%).

The problem for individual investors is that the Barclays Capital U.S. Aggregate Bond Index contains several thousand different individual bonds, so there is no way you can exactly match this in your own portfolio. The next best thing is the Vanguard Total Bond Market Index Fund (VBMFX), which tracks this index as its goal. The fund has succeeded in its goal since its inception in 1986, except for the expense ratio of 0.19% per year, which is far better (i.e., lower) than the 1% that is more typical of bond mutual funds. Vanguard's Total Bond Market Index Fund outperformed anywhere from 70% to 93% of available bond funds over one- to ten-year periods through 2/28/2009.[4]

*The first lesson, therefore, is that if you place your bond investments entirely in the Vanguard Total Bond Market Index Fund (VBMFX), you will likely end up better than most bond investors.*

The Vanguard Total Bond Market Index Fund does not impose a sales load and is available directly from Vanguard (www.vanguard.com) with a minimum investment of $3,000. As of 10/2/2009, the SEC yield of the Total Bond Market Index Fund (VBMFX) is 3.5% and the average maturity is 6.8 years.[5] Its worst drawdown has been -6.5%, which occurred during the 1994 bear market for bonds. However, you should note that the Barclays Capital U.S. Aggregate Bond Index itself lost 13% from peak to valley during the high-inflation, rising interest rate environment of 1979–1980 (before the Vanguard fund was in existence). The recurrence of that sort of investment climate cannot be ruled out in the future.

# Swing for the Fences:
# Pimco Total Return Fund

The manager of the Pimco Total Return Fund, Bill Gross, is perhaps the preeminent star in the bond market universe. His strategy has involved moving his fund disproportionately into areas of the bond market where he sees the greatest potential. That has, at different times, meant foreign bonds, as well as all manner of domestic bonds. He also adjusts the maturity of his bond holdings so that when he expects interest rates to rise, his fund will shift into shorter-term bonds, and vice versa.

The Pimco Total Return Fund (PTTRX) has returned an average of 1.6% per year more than the Vanguard Total Bond Market Index Fund (VBMFX) between 9/1/1988 and 3/31/2009 (that is, compounded annual return of 8.7% per year versus 7.1% per year during the 1988–2009 period). This increase in return came at the expense of about 20% more volatility for the Pimco fund, although the worst drawdown for the Pimco Total Return Fund has been similar to that of the usually quieter Vanguard Total Bond Market Index Fund. The reason is that the Pimco manager's bond market timing skills succeeded in reducing risk during the bad bond market climate of 1994. In 2007–2009, Pimco's investors did suffer a greater drawdown (6.7% versus 5.5% for the Vanguard Total Bond Market Index Fund), commensurate with the degree to which the Pimco Total Return Fund has been more volatile than the overall bond market.

The preceding performance results reflect the share class with the lowest expense ratio (0.43%), which is the "institutional class." As an individual investor, you might be able to access the institutional class share through your 401(k) plan or discount brokerage platform. However, many individual investors must content themselves with a higher-expense, lower-returning share. For example, the class A share has an expense ratio of 0.9% per year, and the class B or C shares have a whopping 1.65% per year expense ratio. The added charges for the more expensive shares go to the brokers who sold them to you.

Let's stop for a moment and consider the implications of buying a class B or C share of the Pimco Total Return Fund. Note that because the 1.65% per year expense ratio of these shares exceeds that of the institutional share class by 1.22% per year, these more expensive shares return 1.22% per year less than the most economical offering. Because PTTRX beat the Vanguard Total Bond Market Index Fund (VBMFX) by 1.6% per year, the class B and C versions of Pimco Total Return would have added just 0.4% per year to the performance of the Vanguard fund. When you take into account the greater month-to-month volatility of Pimco Total Return compared with the Vanguard Total Bond Market Index Fund, the class B and C shares are no longer the better bet (assuming that the relative performance results of the past ten years repeat themselves in the future).

*The moral of the story, which cannot be overstated, is that you should never buy class B or class C shares of a mutual fund, and you should never pay an up-front sales charge to buy class A shares. (Some retirement plans allow individual investors to buy class A shares without imposing the up-front, several-percent sales commission that you would pay to buy the same shares through a commission brokerage firm.)*

# The Safest of the Safe: FPA New Income and SIT U.S. Government Securities

Diversified bond fund investments have been very safe since the late 1980s, and if there were no examples of bond risk greater than what has occurred since then, bond investors could rest easy. Unfortunately, we have already seen that during periods of rising inflation and interest rates as we experienced in the late 1970s, bonds do very poorly. A replay of the 1970s to at least some extent certainly cannot be ruled out.

If you are concerned about future bond risks, there are two mutual funds whose managers have superior records of risk control: FPA New Income (FPNIX) and SIT U.S. Government Securities (SNGVX). These funds move into short-term Treasury debt when conditions darken. From 1988 to 2009, the worst drawdown for the SIT fund was just 2%, whereas that of the FPA fund was just 4%. Nonetheless, in the low-rate environment of late 2009, the SEC yield on SIT U.S. Government Securities was an attractive 4.8%, while FPA New Income was paying income distributions at a rate of 3% at a time when most money markets were paying virtually nothing. (FPA New Income does not disclose its SEC yield.[6]

# Conclusion

Carefully selected bond mutual funds can be valuable tools for you and are almost mandatory if you have less than $25,000 to invest in your bond portfolio. Bond mutual funds can also be desirable if you want the yield you can get from longer-term bonds but want the freedom to access some or all of your investment in the nearer term. But beware—most bond funds are not worth your trouble, especially those that come with an up-front or back-end sales load or funds with high-expense share classes such as class C shares.

Specific taxable bond mutual funds that are worthy of your consideration (if they meet your objectives) include Pimco Total Return (PTTRX) and the Vanguard Total Bond Market Index Fund (VBMFX). Funds that have been extremely safe and which might be more profitable alternatives to bank CDs or to leaving significant sums in a money market include FPA New Income (FPNIX) and SIT

U.S. Government Securities (SNGVX). This is obviously not an exhaustive list, and you might be able to locate other superior bond funds by looking for funds with below-average expenses that had below-average losses during previous bond bear markets, including 1994, 1999, and, in the case of corporate bonds, 2002 and 2008. Chapter 8, "Municipal Bonds—Keep the Taxman at Bay," lists recommended mutual funds that invest in tax-free bonds.

# Appendix:
# A Word of Caution about Bond ETFs

Exchange-traded funds (ETFs) are a special type of mutual fund whose shares trade like stocks throughout the day. In contrast, conventional open-end mutual fund shares trade only once at the end of each day. ETF shareholders trade with each other at the prevailing market price, whereas open-end mutual fund shareholders purchase or redeem shares from the mutual fund company, all at the same daily price.

At first glance, ETFs would seem ideally suited for bond investors because they have lower expense ratios than almost all mutual funds, which leaves more interest income available to pay to shareholders. Bond ETFs now offer investors exposure to many different areas of the bond market, including Treasuries, mortgage-backed bonds (agency debt), corporate investment-grade bonds, high-yield bonds, and municipal bonds.

The problem with many bond ETFs is that their prices have displayed big short-term fluctuations that bond fund investors have not experienced. For example, Figure 5–1 shows two years' total return history for three investments that all track the same benchmark (Barclays U.S. Aggregate Bond Index): the Vanguard Total Bond

Market Index Fund (VBMFX), the iShares Barclay's U.S. Aggregate Bond Index ETF (AGG), and the Vanguard Total Bond Market Index ETF (BND).

Note that before August 2008, all three investments behaved pretty much the same, as you would expect. However, starting in August 2008, the bond market became much more volatile than usual as the financial crisis developed. During this period, price swings in the two bond ETFs shown in Figure 5–1 were far larger than price swings in the Vanguard Total Bond Market Index Fund (VBMFX). The larger ETF price swings were random, making the ETFs riskier than the bond fund without being more profitable.

The bond fund itself holds over 3,800 different bonds, and each day's share price reflects the weighted average of every one of those bonds regardless of how many investors want to buy or redeem shares that day. Vanguard's bond ETF (BND) also has 3,800 bonds, but unlike the mutual fund, the ETF share price reflects the balance of supply and demand for the shares. Normally, there are financial firms (called authorized participants) who buy or sell ETF shares and baskets of the underlying bonds to capitalize on discrepancies between the two. The result is that ETF share prices and the value of the underlying basket of securities usually stay close to each other. However, during volatile markets, this mechanism did not function, and ETF share prices were all over the map even as the mutual fund (VBMFX) moved more smoothly.

The iShares Barclay's Aggregate Bond Index ETF (AGG) has only 175 different bonds in it (as of 4/9/09). As you can see from Figure 5–1, despite this vastly smaller number of bonds, AGG has done a good job of tracking an index with 9,000 bonds. But again, during abnormally volatile markets, all bets are off.

If you happen to buy one of these bond ETFs at the time of an unusually large price decline, or sell at the time of an unusual price spike, then ETFs could prove more profitable than bond mutual funds. However, most of the time the potential for unusual price spikes up or down simply represents an unwelcome dose of added risk. This risk of market volatility has applied to other bond ETFs as well, not just the total bond market ETFs. ETFs that hold less liquid types of bonds (e.g., high yields, municipals, investment-grade corporates) are especially vulnerable. Overall, in the case of bond ETFs, the disadvantages of trading costs (bid-ask spread and brokerage commission) and price risk outweigh the yield advantages. You should be very wary of bond ETFs: This is one area where certain conventional mutual funds are likely to be superior.

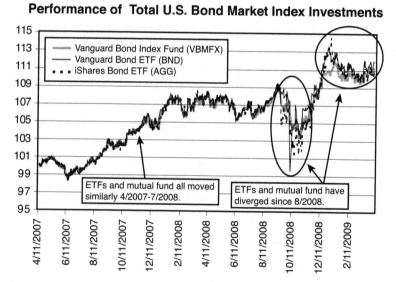

**Performance of Total U.S. Bond Market Index Investments**

Legend:
- Vanguard Bond Index Fund (VBMFX)
- Vanguard Bond ETF (BND)
- iShares Bond ETF (AGG)

ETFs and mutual fund all moved similarly 4/2007-7/2008.

ETFs and mutual fund have diverged since 8/2008.

**Figure 5-1** *Performance of three investments that track the Barclay's U.S. Aggregate Bond Market Index, 2007–2009*

## chapter 6

# The Safest Investment There Is—Treasury Inflation-Protected Securities (TIPS)

Inflation is the enemy of the bond investor and is your enemy if you are living on a fixed income. Once you lock in a rate of return by buying a bond, if prices rise faster than your investment is growing, you are stuck. Fortunately, the federal government offers you a guaranteed way to beat inflation with no risk of losing any money: Treasury Inflation-Protected Securities (TIPS), also known as inflation-indexed Treasury notes (or bonds). This chapter explains how TIPS work and how you can best use them.

## How TIPS Work

Most bonds are issued and later redeemed in units of $1,000. TIPS work differently: Although they are issued in units of $1,000, the principal value of the bonds, rather than staying at $1,000 throughout the life of the bonds, increases in parallel with the Consumer Price Index.[1] This means that if you bought an inflation-indexed Treasury bond when issued, and during the life of the bond, consumer prices rose 10%, then at maturity you will receive $1,100, not the usual $1,000. If prices had risen by 15%, then you would get $1,150 at maturity. If prices had fallen during the life of the bond, you would still get $1,000 at maturity.

If you buy or sell TIPS sometime between when they are issued and when they mature, the amount you pay is calculated based on the original $1,000 issue price adjusted for the inflation that occurred since issue. The Treasury keeps track of how the Consumer Price Index has fluctuated since the issuance of every one of its different TIPS. So, for example, if you buy a previously issued inflation-indexed Treasury bond and prices have already increased 5% since it was issued, you will pay for $1,050 in bond principal, not $1,000. If prices rise another 2% and you sell, the amount you receive will be 2% higher than $1,050, or $1,071 (assuming no change in interest rates).

Note that if you buy a newly issued inflation-indexed Treasury bond, you are guaranteed to receive at least $1,000/bond at maturity even if prices decline during the life of the bond (which is very unlikely). However, if you sell an inflation-indexed bond before maturity and prices have declined during the period you owned it, you would likely suffer a capital loss.

In addition to keeping up with inflation, TIPS also pay a fixed *rate* of interest just like other bonds. However, the coupon interest payments from TIPS are not constant throughout the life of the bond. Rather, they are a fixed *percentage* of the current principal value. You can see this most easily with an example.

Suppose you buy an inflation-indexed Treasury bond at issuance for $1,000 with a coupon of 2%. This means that the initial rate of cash interest will be $20/year, which is 2% of $1,000. However, once consumer prices have risen 10%, the principal value of the bond will have increased to $1,100. At that point, the 2% coupon payment is 2% of $1,100, or $22/year. So not only does the principal value of your bond increase with inflation, but your interest does too. As we discussed in Chapter 2, "Basics of Bond Investments," this is the ideal investment: no risk of default and a stream of investment income that keeps pace with inflation. The only other source of retirement income that provides these benefits is Social Security.

In fact, TIPS would be the ideal investment for retirees except for two big problems: low returns and taxes. TIPS generally pay 1.0%–2.0% above inflation, which means that if you do not want to deplete the purchasing power of your investments, you are limited to spending just that 1.0%–2.0% level of interest income. Most of us have not saved enough to get by on that little.

The tax problem for those of you who would hold TIPS in taxable accounts is that the amount by which your bond principal is adjusted for inflation counts as interest income, the same as if you had received it as a cash coupon payment. However, principal adjustments are not cash in your pocket. Rather, they are embedded in the value of your bonds. You don't see any gains from an increase in principal until you sell your bonds or until they mature.

In a setting of high inflation, you could actually end up owing more in taxes than you collect in coupon payments. For example, if you hold a 2% TIPS and are in a 40% combined federal/state tax bracket, then in a year when inflation is 3%, you would owe taxes as follows: 40% of the 2% in coupon payments and 40% of the 3% inflation adjustment. The combined tax burden equals 2% of the principal value of your bonds (that is, $40\% \times 2\% + 40\% \times 3\% = 2\%$). This means that you must turn over your entire coupon payment as taxes. In a year when inflation exceeds 3%, you would owe more than you collected.

There are low-cost mutual funds and ETFs that can help you avoid the risk of owing taxes that exceed the amount of cash interest. These funds invest in the entire range of TIPS that have been issued. Two examples are the Vanguard Inflation-Protected Securities Fund (VIPSX) and the iShares Barclays TIPS Bond ETF (TIP). Both of these have low expense ratios: 0.25% for the Vanguard fund and just 0.2% for the TIPS ETF by iShares. The reason why owning TIPS through an ETF or mutual fund avoids a cash-flow problem is that these funds must make taxable distributions of all taxable gains to their shareholders, regardless of whether those taxable gains are in the form of coupon interest or in the form of an inflation adjustment to the principal value of TIPS.

Normally, when you buy a mutual fund such as Vanguard's TIPS fund (VIPSX), the distribution is in the form of additional shares of the fund. The fund sends you a "form 1099" each year (typically by early February) declaring the amount of taxable distribution you received. It is up to you to find the cash to pay the taxes due, either by selling fund shares or by raising the cash elsewhere. However, mutual funds do give you the option of receiving taxable distributions in cash rather than in the form of additional fund shares. ETFs generally pay cash as the default option. You will receive cash from the fund or ETF even though the fund itself did not get any cash as the result of an increase in the principal of the TIPS in the fund's portfolio. It becomes the fund's task to raise the cash necessary to pay you, and not yours. The bottom line is that if you elect to receive taxable distributions from a TIPS fund in cash, you will never owe more taxes than the amount of cash you receive.

Unfortunately, if you own a fund of TIPS, you lose the absolute guarantee of knowing that your investment will beat inflation over a certain time period. If TIPS prices fall during the period you own a TIPS fund, the losses could exceed the interest you receive. But if you own individual TIPS, you can guarantee that at maturity, each inflation-indexed bond will have returned a profit that exceeds inflation. For this reason, I do not recommend owning TIPS funds as a long-term investment.

*Instead, the best solution for the taxation of TIPS is to hold them in IRA or other tax-deferred accounts.* Then you would not owe taxes on any principal adjustment until you actually took a taxable distribution of your earnings. In fact, the absolute best solution is to own TIPS within a Roth IRA. That way, you will not owe any taxes on the returns from TIPS. *Holding TIPS within a Roth IRA is the only way to keep ahead of inflation after taxes with no risk.*

2009–2010 is a good time to think about contributing to a Roth IRA if you are eligible. Tax cuts enacted during the presidency of George W. Bush are set to expire on 1/1/2011 in the absence of specific legislation to extend them. With federal deficits in record territory for peacetime, it is all but certain that income tax rates will be rising one way or another. The higher the income tax rate, the harder it is to accumulate after-tax money to contribute to a Roth IRA and the more valuable assets within an existing Roth IRA become. Add as much as you can to your Roth IRAs before income tax rates go up.

## HOW MUCH CAN YOU ADD TO A ROTH IRA?

According to IRS Publication 590 "Individual Retirement Arrangements," available on www.irs.gov, you can contribute a maximum of $5,000 per year to a Roth IRA before age 50, and $6,000 per year if you are older. However, you can contribute the maximum only if your "modified adjusted gross income" for 2009 falls below $105,000 if you are filing singly or $166,000 if you file jointly.

These contribution limits are reduced for taxpayers who earn more than these amounts. If as a single filer you earn between $105,000 and $120,000 (or between $166,000 and $176,000 as a joint filer), the government allows you to contribute something less than the maximum amount to a Roth IRA. If you earn more than $120,000 as a single filer or $176,000 as a joint filer, you cannot contribute anything at all to a Roth IRA for 2009.

## TIPS Prices Fluctuate when Interest Rates Change, Similar to Regular Bonds

Suppose you buy an inflation-indexed Treasury note with a fixed interest rate of 2% and immediately thereafter, the demand for TIPS evaporates so that investors demand a fixed rate of 2.5%. In this case, the value of your bond falls, the same as would happen to any bond when interest rates rise. In general, TIPS prices move in the same direction as the prices of regular Treasury bonds of similar maturities, at least from day to day and week to week: If the yield on ten-year regular Treasury notes rises, the odds are good that the fixed interest rate on ten-year TIPS has also risen at the same time, although perhaps not by exactly the same amount.

When you buy a regular bond and hold it until maturity, your investment return is predetermined. The same is true of TIPS: If you hold it until maturity, the amount of your investment return above inflation is determined at the time of purchase. However, if you sell a regular bond or an inflation-indexed Treasury bond before maturity, there is no guarantee how much you will earn.

As with regular bonds, if you buy a mutual fund that holds TIPS, there is no single maturity date. Rather, the portfolio of the fund is constantly evolving, and you cannot predict your future returns at the time of purchase the way you can when you buy an individual bond.

*The bottom line is that if you buy an inflation-indexed Treasury note at issue and hold it until maturity in a tax-deferred account, you are guaranteed to beat inflation with no risk of default. Individual TIPS are a great investment for investors who do not want to actively manage their holdings. You simply buy TIPS and hold them until maturity.*

# Market Prices for Previously Issued TIPS: Trickier Than You Might Expect

If you look up the price of a previously issued Treasury note, the price quote you see reflects a fraction of par value. So, for example, you could have looked up the price of the January 2014 1.75% Treasury note in the 4/27/09 issue of Barron's (a weekly financial newspaper). You would have found the quote of 99 10/32, which means that bond dealers could buy this Treasury note for $993.125. (You would have to pay more as an individual.) Barron's also reported that the yield to maturity of this bond was 1.9%. The reason that the bond is trading below par is that interest rates rose (from 1.75% to 1.9%) since the time the bond was issued. Only a change in interest rates changes the price of outstanding Treasuries.

To summarize: Quotes for regular Treasury notes (in Barron's) appear as shown in Table 6–1.

Table 6–1   *Sample Quotation for a Regular Treasury Note*

| Coupon Rate | Maturity Date (Month/Year) | Bid Price | Ask Price | Price Change from Previous Period | Yield to Maturity (Based on Ask Price) |
|---|---|---|---|---|---|
| 1.75% | January 2014 | 99 9/32 | 99 10/32 | -9/32 | 1.90% |

However, we have seen that either of two distinct events can affect the price of previously issued TIPS: a change in interest rates or a change in the Consumer Price Index. Each of these events is reported separately.

The price quote on an inflation-indexed Treasury note reflects the fraction of par value that the bond is worth at prevailing interest rates. For example, in the April 27, 2009, Barron's, the January 2016 TIPS with a coupon of 2% was quoted at 102 17/32 (102.53125). The fact that the bond is trading above par means that interest rates have fallen below 2% since the bond was issued. This means that this bond is quoted at 102.53125% of par value. But unlike other bonds, par value is not $1,000. Barron's also reports what the par value has grown to since issue, in this case $1051. So if you wanted to buy this bond on the secondary market, you would have to pay $1051 × 1.0253125 = $1077.603. In addition to the $1,077.603 per bond, as a practical matter you would have to pay the interest that accrued since the last coupon payment and you would have to pay a markup to the dealer that sold you the bond.

If you hold an inflation-indexed Treasury note in your brokerage account, your statements will likely not reflect the increase in principal since the bond was issued. In the previous example, the bond that you could sell for $1077.60 would likely appear on your statement as 102.53. To evaluate the actual price of your bond, you would have to look it up in Barron's. Alternatively, you could use the market quote from your brokerage statement and multiply that by the principal value of your bond, which is available online at www.savingsbonds.gov.

To summarize: Quotes for TIPS would appear (in Barron's, for example) as shown in Table 6–2.

Table 6–2    *Sample Quotation for a Treasury Inflation-Protected Security*

| Coupon Rate | Maturity Date (Month/ Year) | Bid Price | Ask Price | Price Change from Previous Period | Yield to Maturity Above Inflation | Accrued Principal per Bond ($) |
|---|---|---|---|---|---|---|
| 2.00% | January 2016 | 102 16/32 | 102 17/32 | +9/32 | 1.60% | 1051 |

Note that there is an additional column to report the current principal of each TIPS. In the case of regular bonds, the current principal is always $1,000 and, therefore, is not reported.

# How to Buy TIPS

I recommend buying only individual TIPS. You can do this through your broker, or directly from the Treasury at www.savingsbonds.gov. Your broker can buy newly issued TIPS for you at one of the quarterly auctions (for an additional fee), or can buy previously issued TIPS for you on the secondary market (the same way you would obtain other bonds). The best source of information about TIPS (including upcoming auction dates and updated principal values for existing TIPS) is on the Treasury Web site: www.savingsbonds.gov/indiv/ research/indepth/ tips/res_tips_faq.htm. The easiest way to get to this Web site (at least as of 4/12/09) is to do a Google search for "individual TIPS FAQs."

# What Is a Good Yield for TIPS?

To decide whether TIPS offer a good value, it helps to be familiar with historical precedent. Figure 6–1 shows the range of fixed yields on ten-year TIPS from 2003 to 2009.[2] During these six years, the fixed yield on ten-year TIPS ranged from 1% to 3%, with an average of 2%. By the standards of recent history, therefore, *newly issued ten-year TIPS represents an above-average value if its fixed yield is at least 2%*. I believe that adopting this rule of thumb will serve you well, even though you might have to wait for months or even a couple of years to get the bargain you want.

When TIPS were first issued in 1997, deflation was the threat that policymakers and investors feared. Inflation was not on the horizon. As a result, the fixed yields on TIPS were initially very high, ranging from 3% to 4% from 1997 to 1999. Those were the days. If the real (fixed) yield on a newly issued ten-year TIPS ever gets back above 3%, that would be a strong indication to buy them. You could even buy the TIPS ETF (ticker symbol TIP) as a trading vehicle with real yields at that level, holding until real yields slip back below 2%.

Note that the yields on TIPS issued years ago are frequently higher than newly issued TIPS. That is because newly issued TIPS are guaranteed not to lose principal even in the event of deflation (falling prices) during the life of the bond. However, an old inflation-indexed Treasury note whose principal already reflects significant accrued inflation does pose the risk that the bond will lose the accrued principal if prices fall after you buy the bond. The government guarantees buyers of new TIPS that the principal at maturity will not drop below $1,000/bond, but there is no guarantee that the principal on a bond that already exceeds $1,000 will not return to the original $1,000 level.

**10-Year TIPS Real Yield**

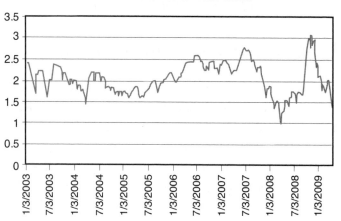

Figure 6–1    *Real yield on the ten-year TIPS, 2003–2009*

Lastly, it should be of comfort to TIPS investors to know that from 2003 to 2009, the total interest paid on ten-year TIPS (i.e., fixed rate plus the amount of inflation) did exceed the interest paid on regular ten-year Treasury notes. During this period, ten-year TIPS paid an average of 2% per year above inflation (as we already saw in Figure 6–1), whereas the coupon payments on regular ten-year Treasury notes amounted to just 1.3% per year above inflation.

If you want to know the latest information about what real (fixed) yields TIPS of different maturities are offering, you can visit the U.S. Treasury Web site at www.ustreas.gov/offices/domestic-finance/debt-management/interest-rate/real_yield.shtml.[3]

# Should You Invest in TIPS or Invest in Corporates?

There exists a constant demand for regular Treasury notes by foreign central banks and other institutional buyers that are relatively insensitive to the level of interest rates. Therefore, it seems reasonable to assume that TIPS will usually offer a better return to the individual investor than will conventional Treasury notes.

The harder question for you is whether TIPS will serve you better than investment-grade corporate bonds. TIPS are certainly safer, but will they pay you as much interest? As of late 2009, it appears that some corporate bonds offer a higher potential return. If you buy ten-year TIPS at a fixed rate of 1.1% and if inflation averages 4% per year in the future, your return will be 5.1% per year from the TIPS. If you can find ten-year corporate bonds that pay more than 5.1% per year, they will probably be more profitable for you.

Note that most financial planners assume that inflation will average less than 4% per year. In 2009–2010, it does indeed appear that inflation will come in at less than 4% per year. However, you should remember that 4% has been the average inflation rate since the end of World War II, largely due to the inflationary 1970s. The levels of deficit spending and currency creation that occurred in 2009 and are projected to continue in 2010 and beyond are unprecedented (at least during peacetime), and your planning should not exclude the possibility that these measures will rekindle inflation in the coming decade as well.

## A SAVINGS BOND ALTERNATIVE TO TIPS

We have seen that TIPS are the ultimate safe investment if held until maturity. However, the impact of taxes makes TIPS less appealing in taxable accounts. There is a possible solution: Series I Savings Bonds, also called I-bonds.

I-bonds work the same way as TIPS: They pay a fixed percentage that you know when you buy the bonds, and in addition, they pay you according to how much inflation has accrued during the time.

The biggest advantage of I-bonds is that the interest they pay is tax-deferred until you redeem your bonds. That means that you will never be in a situation where the taxes you owe on your I-bonds could exceed the cash you received in interest.

The other advantage of I-bonds is that *you* decide when to redeem them, with the only restrictions being that you do have to hold them for a minimum of five years, and you will not earn interest after 30 years. (If you try to cash in an I-bond before five years, you will be socked with a penalty of three months' interest.) Because you get to decide when to redeem your I-bonds, you can hold them for as long as interest rates remain lower than what your I-bond is paying, and you can cash them in as soon as a more advantageous investment comes along.

The big disadvantage of I-bonds is that they sometimes pay far less than TIPS. The Treasury sets the real rate every six months, on May 1 and November 1. When you buy I-bonds, you are locked in at whatever fixed rate the Treasury has placed in effect. For example, I-bonds purchased between 11/1/2009 and 4/30/2010 will pay a fixed rate of 0.3% per year. By way of comparison, five-year TIPS are paying 0.5%–0.7%, and ten-year TIPS are paying 1.1%–1.2% above inflation as of November 2009.

There is a reason why the government is so stingy with I-bonds. The Treasury is committed to the rate for six months after publishing it regardless of what the bond market does. If market rates fall, investors could theoretically achieve an above-market rate with no risk by purchasing I-bonds. This risk, as well as the flexibility of the bond buyer to redeem his bonds whenever it is advantageous to do so, account for the smaller yield on I-bonds. The government must have felt it got a raw deal because it has reduced the maximum amount of I-bonds you can purchase in any year from $30,000 in the past to just $5,000 now.

As a rule of thumb, I-bonds are attractive relative to TIPS if the I-bond fixed yield is within 0.5% of the fixed yield on a newly issued ten-year TIPS. I-bonds were excellent investments for individuals in years past. As of late 2009, they are not attractive, but if the bond market settles down, perhaps they will again be a good deal for the individual investor with $5,000 to invest at no risk.

You buy I-bonds through your local bank. The bank withdraws the funds directly from your account and forwards them to the government. A few weeks later, you will receive your paper I-bonds in the mail. You can also receive your bonds electronically in your Treasury Direct account. You can get more information about I-bonds at the Treasury Direct Web site, www.treasurydirect.gov/indiv/research/indepth/ibonds/res_ibonds.htm.

## Conclusion

The recommended strategy for TIPS is to buy newly issued ten-year TIPS only at real yields of at least 2%. The return you can reasonably expect (although there are no guarantees) from such bonds should turn out to be 5%–6% per year, better than what conventional ten-year Treasury notes have promised in recent years. No other bond investment is as safe as TIPS in terms of both default risk (none) and inflation risk (none).

TIPS are likely to be more profitable for you than regular Treasuries of the same maturity, assuming that you hold the bond for its entire life. The experience of the bond markets since 1960 suggests that a diversified portfolio of investment-grade corporate bonds could be more profitable (but riskier) than TIPS only if the difference between the corporate bond yield and the TIPS real yield exceeds 4%.

# chapter 7

# High-Yield Bond Funds—Earn the Best Yields Available while Managing the Risks

Wouldn't it be great to get 8% per year or more in interest income from a bond mutual fund? This is not idle fantasy at a time when the average investment-grade bond is paying just 4%. You can get very juicy yields if you are willing to bear the credit risk of high-yield bonds, or junk bonds, which represent roughly the bottom sixth of the bond market in terms of creditworthiness. Of course, bond funds that pay 8% in a 4% world are risky, and they are not good investments all the time. In this chapter, you learn how to recognize propitious times to reach for the yield of high-yield bond mutual funds, and when to stay away.

## The Challenge of High-Yield Bond Funds

Figure 7–1 shows the growth of $100 in a hypothetical investment in the Barclay's U.S. Aggregate Bond Index and in the average of corporate high-yield bond funds in the Mutual Fund Expert database.[1] During the 33.25 years of data shown, U.S. investment-grade bonds returned 8.4% per year with a worst drawdown of 13%, whereas the average of high-yield bond funds returned 7.9% per year with a worst drawdown of 32%.

The first question that should enter your mind at this point is why it is worth bothering with high-yield bond funds at all. Historically, they have had lower returns and higher risk compared with investment-grade bond funds. There is a two-part answer. First, interest rates for investment-grade bonds were much higher historically than is now the case in 2009. This means that future potential returns from investment-grade bonds are far more modest than the returns they generated in the 1980s and 1990s. On the other hand, junk bond yields are close to average by historical standards, which means that as the United States emerges from the 2008–2009 recession, the return potential for junk bonds is as attractive as it has been historically. Second, as we examine in more detail in the section "Risk Management: The Stop Loss," you can follow a simple strategy to boost returns and cut risk in high-yield bond funds.

There are three major bear market periods for high-yield bonds circled in Figure 7–1: 1989–1990, 1998–2002, and 2007–2008. The rest of the time, high-yield bonds kept pace with or outperformed investment-grade bonds. Each of these periods of high-yield bond weakness occurred in the setting of recessions, which is logical if you think about it. During periods of economic growth, even marginal companies that have borrowed too much might get by. However, recessions shake out the weaker, more vulnerable players that are disproportionately represented among high-yield bond issuers.

Think about the implications of Figure 7–1: Just three periods of decline in the high-yield bond market account for virtually all of the additional risk in this type of bond compared with investment-grade bonds. These relatively infrequent but major market declines also wiped out the return advantage that high-yield bonds would have had over investment-grade bonds by virtue of the higher interest they pay. The moral of the story is that if you are going to invest in high-yield bond funds in search of their attractive yields, you must have a strategy to deal with the severe bear markets that afflict them every few years.

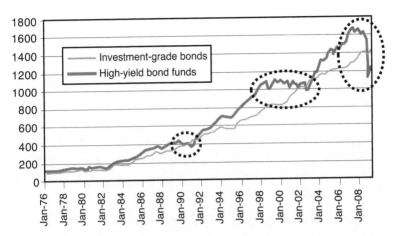

**Figure 7–1** *Hypothetical growth of $100 in high-yield bond funds or in U.S. investment-grade bonds (Barclay's U.S. Aggregate Bond Index), 1976–2009*

# Who Should Avoid High-Yield Bond Funds

The data in Figure 7–1 demonstrates that high-yield bond funds are simply not suitable as buy-and-hold investments, period. Buy-and-hold investors have forfeited years of gains during every recession. It is easy to find investment professionals to tell you that you cannot time the market, that you must invest for the long term, that markets always recover, and so forth. When it comes to high-yield bond funds, the conventional wisdom is wrong. The only way to invest in high-yield bond funds is to check up on your investments regularly and to move to cash at an early sign of potential trouble.

If you do not want to evaluate your bond investments at least once a month, or if you have trouble making the decision to sell, or if you believe only in buying and holding (and praying), then don't invest in high-yield bond funds. You can find many other investment strategies in this book that can work for you. High-yield bond funds are only for active investors (although the amount of activity is minimal).

# Risk Management: The Stop Loss

One of the simplest ways of controlling your investment risk is simply to sell after your investments have fallen by a predetermined percentage from their last peak value. For example, if you own shares in a high-yield bond fund, you might resolve to check the value of those shares (including reinvested interest distributions) at the end of each month, and to sell your shares any time they lose 3% of their most recent peak value. The 3% loss that triggers your decision to sell is called a stop loss.

As an example of how this would work, suppose you invest $9,000 in a high-yield bond fund. The 3% stop loss means that if your initial investment loses $270 (which is 3% of $9,000), you move all your shares to cash. Suppose instead that your $9,000 shrinks to $8,800. This decline does not trigger the sale. Next suppose that the $8,800 grows to $10,000. Now, the new criterion to sell requires your investment to lose 3% from its last high point—so, because of the growth that has occurred, you sell only if your $10,000 loses 3% ($300). In other words, you sell only when your shares drop below $9,700.

The nice thing about this method of risk control is that if you make more than 3%, you have a chance to lock in at least some of those gains. In the preceding example, you bought shares for $9,000 and, after gaining $1,000, your plan is to sell only after they fall below $9,700. That means that you are likely to enjoy gains of approximately $700 when you close out the trade.

But even with a stop loss, nothing is guaranteed. First, if you are checking your investments only once a month, it is possible that your losses will exceed 3%. For example, in June 2008, the average high-yield bond fund lost 2.4%. That would not have triggered a sale, so you would wait another month. In July 2008, the average fund lost another 1.5%. The combined losses during this two-month period were 3.9%, which would trigger the sale. This is larger than the 3% amount of your stop loss.

Note that the amount of the stop loss is the *minimum* amount you will lose before closing out your investment. In the hypothetical example of a $9,000 investment that grew to $10,000 at its most recent peak value: If there were a 15% loss in the month following the peak in the value of your shares, you would end up selling your shares for just $8,500. That represents a loss of $500 from the original investment and $1,500 from what you would have collected if you had had the foresight to sell at the peak.

Stop losses have worked especially well with high-yield bond funds in my experience, but many investors also apply them to other types of bond funds and to stock market investments. There is no simple rule to tell you whether or not to use a stop loss. You must analyze how a stop loss would have affected the performance of the particular investment you are considering. Moreover, even if past results suggest that using a stop loss would have improved your performance, there is no guarantee that this risk-control strategy will work as well in the future.

## What to Do after Your Stop Loss Triggers a Sale

Suppose everything works as you hope, and your stop loss leads you to close out your position a small distance from its peak value, locking in a profit. Now you are back where you started: with a pile of cash and a decision to make about how to reinvest it.

A simple strategy is to use a buy stop: When the shares you are following rise by a preset amount off of their last low point, you buy them.

We can continue with the previous example: You invested $9,000, it rose to $10,000 before falling back to $9,700, at which point you closed out your position with a $700 profit. If the investment gods decide to taunt you, your shares will start climbing as soon as you sell. If you use a 3% buy stop, you would reenter your position when the value of the shares rises 3% above $9,700, which is to say, when they exceed $9,991. If you are especially unlucky, the shares might bounce up and down by just over 3%, enough to trigger your decision to sell low and buy back higher time and time again. An illustration of this unfortunate scenario appears in Figure 7–2.

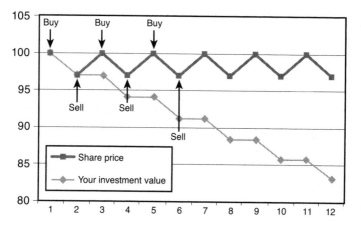

**Figure 7–2** *Losses that would result from using buy stops and stop losses to trade a range-bound investment*

On the other hand, if fortune is on your side, the value of the shares you sold at $9,700 might continue to fall all the way back to $9,000 or even lower. Regardless of how far they fall, your job is to evaluate them each month and reenter the shares with your $9,700 as soon as the shares rise 3% off of the most recent month-end low. Figure 7–3 shows an example of where the use of buy stops and stop losses would be successful in reducing your risk and generating profits even when buying and holding the shares would have produced a loss.

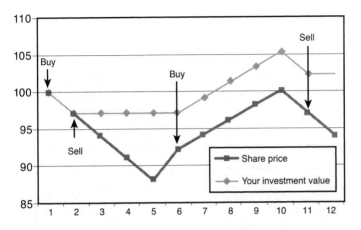

**Figure 7-3**  *Profits that would result from using buy stops and stop losses to trade an investment with strong price trends*

You can see in the previous examples that using buy stops and stop losses only works for investments where the size of the trend is significantly larger than the size of your stops. Fortunately, high-yield bond funds have usually behaved this way. Many stock market investments, unfortunately, have not.

## Results with Some Actual High-Yield Bond Funds

Let's see how using a 3% threshold for selling and repurchasing would have worked with a real high-yield bond fund. Figure 7–4 shows the results that would have been obtained using the Delaware Delchester fund (DETWX). Although there were advantages to using buy and sell stops throughout the 20.5 years shown, the big benefits accrued during the past two high-yield bond bear markets.

Buying and holding Delaware Delchester throughout the period shown (1988–2009) would have returned you 4.3% per year with a 40% drawdown. That was less than the return from risk-free three-month Treasury bills. On the other hand, selling the fund after a 3% decline from a peak, and buying back after a 3% gain off of a trough would have required just 20 transactions (10 buys and 10 sells). The results would have been an annual compounded gain of 7.2% per year with a drawdown of 17%. These results do not include taxes or transaction costs. Nor do they include money market interest you would have earned during the periods when you were not invested in the mutual fund itself.

**Delaware Delchester (DETWX) Total Returns, 1988-2009**

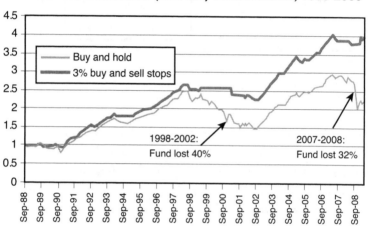

**Figure 7–4** *Total returns from Delaware Delchester, 1988–2009, either buying and holding or trading with 3% buy and sell stops evaluated once a month*

Let's look at the results with another fund, the venerable Northeast Investors Trust (NTHEX), which, founded in 1950, is one of the earliest high-yield bond funds. Until 2007, Northeast Investors Trust had a superlative track record, avoiding drawdowns over 15%. However, in 2007–2008, that excellent prior safety record came to naught as the fund lost 46% of its value. From 1988 to 2009, the fund gained 4.6% per year. If you had used the 3% buy- and sell-stop strategy described here, your returns would have been higher (6.7%) and your risk much lower (15% drawdown). These results are shown graphically in Figure 7–5. As with Delaware Delchester, utilizing 3% monthly buy and sell stops for Northeast Investors Trust would have entailed making 20 transactions (10 buys and 10 sells) during the 20+ years shown.

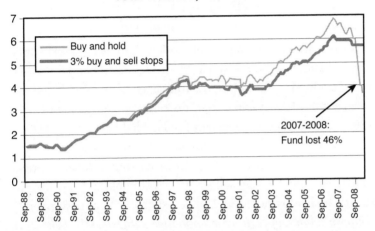

**Northeast Investors Trust (NTHEX)**
**Total Returns, 1988-2009**

**Figure 7-5** *Total returns from Northeast Investors Trust, 1988–2009, either buying and holding or trading with 3% buy and sell stops evaluated once a month*

My experience is that the buy-stop/sell-stop strategy works with most open-end high-yield bond mutual funds, although the extent to which you can add to returns and/or reduce risk compared with buying and holding will vary from fund to fund.

However, you should not use this strategy to trade closed-end high-yield bond funds or high-yield bond ETFs such as the iShares iBoxx $ High Yield Bond ETF (HYG) or the SPDR Barclays High Yield Bond ETF (JNK). As we discussed in Chapter 5, "Bond Mutual Funds—Where the Best Places Are for Your One-Stop Shopping," bond ETFs move less smoothly than bond mutual funds, which undermines any trading strategy (including this one) that attempts to catch up with trends that have already begun.

## Why Not Evaluate More Frequently Than Once a Month?

The 3% buy- and sell-stop strategy proposed here generally works even better if you evaluate the value of your bond fund shares once a week rather than once a month. Indeed, in our own money management practice, we use weekly high-yield bond fund data (with additional refinements to the strategy described here).

However, there is an important roadblock to using weekly price data to evaluate buy and sell stops. Many high-yield bond funds and many mutual fund platforms impose trading restrictions to discourage active investors. For example, one discount brokerage imposed its own 2% early redemption fee on any fund not held for at least 90 days. Most of the time, even if you reevaluate your funds each week, you will not be trading nearly that often. However, during volatile periods when following the buy and sell stops is most important, any fee that limits your ability to trade would be devastating to your performance. *The imposition of any early redemption fee outweighs the benefits of following a weekly system.*

If you have the time and inclination to evaluate buy or sell stops on a weekly rather than a monthly basis, part of the work required will include identifying high-yield bond funds and trading platforms that permit the strategy. That might require utilizing different funds on subsequent trades. The rules in high-yield bond funds' prospectuses should guide you.

One final note: You might wonder if you could get by evaluating your high-yield bond funds less frequently than once a month. This is possible,[2] but the results of a monthly or weekly strategy have been superior, especially in terms of greater safety, and are worth the effort.

## Why Not Just Avoid High-Yield Bonds during Recessions?

There are two reasons why simply watching the financial news for announcements that a recession has begun or ended would not work as signals to sell or buy high-yield bond funds. First, the start and end dates of recessions are recognized months after the fact—too late to use the information to make investment decisions. For example, the National Bureau of Economic Research (NBER, the definitive analysts of recession start and end dates) did not announce the start of the recession that began in March 2001 until November of that year—the same month in which the 2001 recession ended. More recently, only in late November 2008 did the NBER determine that the 2008–2009 recession had begun on 1/1/2008, which was 11 months after the fact. If you had waited for the NBER to act on your investments, you would have done very poorly. This is not a criticism of the NBER. Their job is to report on economic history, not to help investors make trading decisions in real time.

Second, the financial markets generally anticipate economic changes. So if the economy is destined to fall into recession, high-yield bond prices could well begin to decline before the economy does. This was certainly the case in 2007–2009: High-yield bond prices peaked in mid-2007, months before the recession began and more than a year before the beginning of the recession was recognized. So if you use the sell-stop discipline described here, you might find yourself acting ahead of the news rather than behind it, which, of course, is what you want.

## Individual High-Yield Bonds Are Likely to Be Unsuitable for You

We have seen that the only way to benefit from high-yield bonds over the long term is to sell them at an early stage of a market correction. You can't do this with individual bonds. As difficult as it is to sell individual investment-grade corporate bonds before they mature, which would typically cost you 2% of the proceeds, selling individual junk bonds is even harder. Many individual junk bonds do not trade on any given day, so even getting an accurate valuation for your investment is difficult. Mutual funds hire special companies (called pricing services) just to estimate the daily value of their high-yield bond fund portfolios.

# Conclusion

Historical returns from high-yield bond fund trading have averaged some 7% per year over the long term. Although no future performance can be guaranteed, given the attractive levels of junk bond interest these days, it is reasonable to expect this level of returns to continue once the 2008–2009 recession is on the wane. Bear in mind that high-yield bond funds have not produced consistent returns from year to year, so if you have a better year than you expected, you should save any windfall for a rainy day. In contrast to high-yield bond funds, investment-grade bond returns are likely to be lower in the coming 20 years than they have been during the past 20, simply because we are now in an era of historically low interest rates.

The return potential of high-yield bond funds comes at the price of increased risk. Conservative investors (for whom exposing more than 25% of capital to stocks is too risky) should likewise limit their high-yield bond fund exposure to 25% of their total assets. However, if you are the type of investor who is comfortable placing up to half of your capital into equities, you could easily place half of your bond capital in high-yield bond fund trading, especially if you are able to evaluate the buy- and sell-stop levels on a weekly basis.

# chapter 8

# Municipal Bonds—
# Keep the Taxman at Bay

Nothing is certain but death and taxes. A related certainty is that your taxes will rise in the coming years to pay for the trillions in federal government deficit spending that has already occurred in 2008 and 2009. Fortunately, there is an alternative to paying taxes on your investment gains: municipal (also called tax-exempt) bonds. They are attractive to tax-conscious investors because if you choose carefully, the interest you receive will be yours to keep without having to pay any taxes on it.

However, there are downsides to investing in municipal bonds. For one thing, the amount of interest you receive from taxable corporate bonds is frequently higher than what you would receive from municipal bonds, even after deducting the taxes you would owe. Second, municipal bonds are even less liquid than corporates, which means that if you ever decide to sell a municipal bond before it matures, it could easily cost you several percent of your investment.

Lastly, state and local governments are entering uncharted territory in terms of the financial risks they face. Moreover, state and local governments are not as closely regulated as corporate borrowers.[1] For example, they do not have to account for the hundreds of billions in retirement benefits they have promised to past and future retirees from the government payroll. Retirement benefits already account for a large and growing share of local government budgets, and there is currently no way to control these spiraling costs. That means that the future risks of municipal bond defaults might be greater than anything seen since the 1970s or even worse. On the positive side, if the federal government displays the same largesse toward financially imperiled state and local governments that it has shown toward major financial institutions or the U.S. auto industry, municipal bonds could paradoxically become safer than ever. I recommend being cautious about credit risk when you buy municipal bonds.

In this chapter, you see how to evaluate whether the yield on a municipal bond is attractive compared with the alternatives and how to shop for the best individual bonds. You also see which mutual funds I recommend to overcome the drawbacks of municipal bond investing while reaping the benefits.

# Comparing Apples with Oranges

The first step in evaluating whether a municipal bond is attractive is to know how much tax you would otherwise pay on taxable interest income. Suppose that every additional dollar of taxable interest increases your tax liability by 35 cents. This means that you are in a 35% tax bracket. Armed with this information, you can compare taxable yields to tax-free yields.

Here is an example. Suppose a taxable bond pays 6% per year in interest. This means that you will lose 35% of that 6% to taxes. The tax bite is $35\% \times 6\% = 2.1\%$, leaving $6\% - 2.1\% = 3.9\%$ in interest income to you. So a municipal bond of equal credit rating and maturity would be a better deal for you on an after-tax basis if it pays more than 3.9%.

As of late 2009, Treasury and mortgage-backed yields are so low that they make municipal bonds more remunerative for almost everyone. As an example, in November 2009, 20-year Treasury bonds were yielding 4.2%, whereas 20-year municipal bonds were paying 4.4%. So if you were in the market for the highest yield and were not worried about default risk, municipal bonds would be a no-brainer...if these were the only two choices.

But as a bond investor, you could also choose to invest in taxable investment-grade corporate bonds. In April 2009, the bonds in the Barclays Corporate Bond Index were paying more than 7%, whereas the bonds in the Barclays Municipal Bond Index were yielding just 3.8%. That made investment-grade corporates the better choice for any investor whose tax bracket was under 46%. However, in the months that followed, corporate bond yields fell while municipal bond yields stayed about the same, so that by the summer of 2009 an investor in a 35% tax bracket would have earned the same interest (after taxes) from either the corporate bond index or the municipal bond index. The take-home lesson is that you should check on available corporate bond yields in light of your own tax situation because even after taxes, you might be better off holding taxable bonds.

# Tax-Exempt Mutual Funds Have a Big Hurdle to Clear

We have already seen that municipal bonds pay less interest than taxable bonds, all else being equal. However, municipal bond mutual funds are not less expensive than taxable bond funds: According to Mutual Fund Expert (3/31/09), both types of mutual funds have expense ratios of 1.0%. Mutual fund expenses take a bigger bite out of tax-exempt bond interest than out of taxable bond interest. A simple example demonstrates this.

Suppose that corporate bond yields are 6% per year and municipal bond yields are 4% per year. The investor in the 33% tax bracket would reap the same after-tax yield of 4% per year from either type of bond. Now suppose that these bonds are inside a mutual fund portfolio and that the fund's expense ratio is 1% per year. That would leave 5% per year taxable interest or 3% per year tax-free interest available to the mutual fund shareholders. After paying taxes on 5% interest, the taxable bond investor would be left with a 3.33% after-tax yield, compared with the 3% tax-free yield from the hypothetical municipal bond fund.

In summary, the impact of a 1% expense ratio reduced the after-tax yield on the taxable fund from 4% to 3.33%, a reduction of 0.67%, and reduced the tax-free yield from 4% to 3%. In other words, the 1% mutual fund expense ratio had a more detrimental impact on the municipal bond fund returns than on taxable bond fund returns. The reason is that the extent to which the expense ratio reduced earnings to the taxable fund investor was partially offset by a reduction in taxes owed. There is no analogous reduction in tax liability to offset the reduction in tax-free interest.

# Recommended Tax–Exempt Bond Mutual Funds

If you examine no-load municipal bond funds that have been in existence since 1990 or earlier and look for the ones with the best balance between risk and returns over one-, three-, five-, and ten-year periods, offerings from Vanguard and Fidelity are heavily represented among the most consistent performers. The American Century Tax-Free Bond Fund (TWTIX) also distinguished itself. Table 8–1 lists seven recommended national municipal bond funds. All of them have low expenses of 0.5% per year or less. These funds would be ideal for investors in low-tax states looking to minimize their federal income tax burden. However, if you live in a state with a high income tax, you should also look for funds from these families that hold bonds exempt from your state's income taxes. Note that the information in Table 8–1 will likely change (especially the SEC yield, reported in the table as of November 2009), so you must get up-to-date information about any bond fund at the time you are considering making an investment.

Table 8-1    *Recommended Municipal Bond Funds*

| Mutual Fund | Symbol | SEC Yield | Average Maturity | Worst Losses Since 1990 |
|---|---|---|---|---|
| American Century Tax-Free Bond Fund | TWTIX | 2.9% | 11 years | 1994 drawdown -6.4% 9/11/08–10/16/08 drawdown -8.2% |
| Fidelity Short-Intermediate Municipal Income Fund | FSTFX | 1.7% | 3.6 years | 1994 drawdown -3.5% 9/11/08–10/16/08 drawdown -3.5% |
| Fidelity Intermediate Municipal Income Fund | FLTMX | 2.8% | 5.5 years | 1994 drawdown -9.1% 9/11/08–10/16/08 drawdown -7.0% |
| Fidelity Municipal Income Fund | FHIGX | 3.9% | 8.9 years | 1994 drawdown -14.3% 9/11/08–10/16/08 drawdown -11.9% |
| Vanguard Short-Term Tax Exempt Fund | VWSTX | 0.8% | 1.2 years | 1994 drawdown under 1% 9/11/08–10/16/08 drawdown -1.0% |
| Vanguard Limited-Term Tax Exempt Fund | VMLTX | 1.5% | 2.7 years | 1994 drawdown -2.5% 9/11/08–10/16/08 drawdown -3.2% |
| Vanguard Intermediate-Term Tax Exempt Fund | VWITX | 3.0% | 6.1 years | 1994 drawdown -6.5% 9/11/08–10/16/08 drawdown -8.2% |

The Vanguard Short-Term Tax Exempt Fund (VWSTX) is very well suited for money that you might otherwise consider putting in a taxable CD or leaving in cash for a period of several months or longer because on an after-tax basis, its yield is higher than many other safe investment options and it has been very safe even during the most difficult periods in the municipal bond market.

The intermediate-term mutual funds (American Century Tax-Free Bond Fund, Fidelity Intermediate Municipal Income, and Vanguard Intermediate-Term Tax Exempt) all provide attractive yields compared with what you might get by buying individual municipal bonds of the same maturities as the funds' average. However, if you buy funds, you are not guaranteed a positive return the way you would be if you bought an individual bond and held it until maturity. At this point, there is a better option available to you than these intermediate-term municipal bond funds that are yielding approximately 3.2%–3.4%: the Alpine Ultra Short Tax Optimized Income Fund (ATOIX).

# The Alpine Ultra Short Tax Optimized Income Fund

This fund is yielding 2.0% (as of 9/30/09), which is federal tax free and which compares favorably with the yields available from short-term municipal bonds generally. But it is not the yield that makes this fund unique. Rather, it is the record of safety. Figure 8–1 shows the total return of the fund since its inception late in 2002. Over that period of time, the fund has grown at a compounded (mostly tax-free) rate of 3.4% per year with a worst drawdown of just -1.2%. Just about the only investment where the annual return has far exceeded the worst drawdown has been Treasury bills, and this fund pays much more than they do.

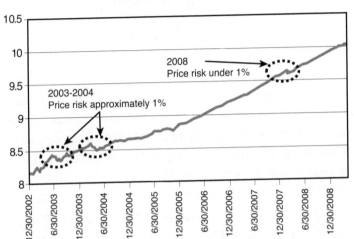

**Figure 8-1** *Total return of the Alpine Ultra Short Tax Optimized Fund (ATOIX), 2003–2009*

The fund's strategy is to invest mainly in floating-rate municipal bonds. The advantage of floating-rate bonds is that there is no price risk when interest rates change—at least not in theory.

Nonetheless, there are potential risks to shareholders. First, the interest rates that variable-rate municipal bonds pay could drop. That would not necessarily affect the price of the fund, but would decrease your returns. Second, the market price of the fund's bonds could drop in the event of another credit crisis. As you can see in Table 8–1, most municipal bond funds suffered significant losses in just the five weeks from 9/11/08 to 10/16/08. Fortunately, those losses have been recouped, but there is no guarantee that this fund will escape the next wave of panic selling to hit the municipal bond market, nor that municipal bonds will recover as quickly as they did after October 2008.

# Earn 7% per Year, Free of Federal Income Tax

The Nuveen High Yield Municipal Bond Fund (NHMAX) has been on my radar for years as a result of its juicy dividend yield and, for most of its history, modest risk. As of 6/30/2009, the fund reported an SEC yield of 8% (assuming you buy the shares without a sales load), but I estimate that the increase in the share price of the fund that has occurred since 6/30/09 has decreased the SEC yield to approximately 7% as of late 2009.[2] The fund is very highly diversified, with more than 1,000 different bonds in its portfolio. This high degree of diversification should help mitigate its risk, although not always, as we will see.

The bad news is that the fund has had to incur lots of risk to achieve its exceptional yield: The average maturity of the bonds in the fund exceeds 22 years, meaning that the fund could potentially have enormous interest rate risk. The average credit rating is the lowest investment grade, BBB-, implying that roughly half of the bonds in the fund are municipal junk bonds, rated below investment grade.

It is remarkable that despite all of these *potential* risks, the Nuveen High Yield Municipal Bond Fund was actually very safe from 2000 to 2006. Figure 8–2 shows that during these years, the value of an investment in the fund pretty much climbed higher with only shallow and brief interruptions.

However, as with so many investments, the chickens came home to roost in 2007–2008. Between May 2007 and December 2008, Nuveen High Yield Municipal Bond Fund lost 45% of its value. (See Figure 8–2.) So once again, investors saw that they need to watch even their historically safe investments so that they can make a timely exit in the event of a sea change in the markets.

## NHMAX Total Return 2000-2009

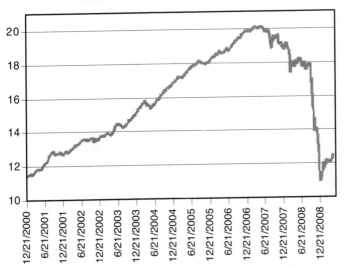

**Figure 8–2** *Total return of Nuveen High Yield Municipal Bond Fund (NHMAX), 12/2000–4/2009*

You can still take advantage of this fund for high levels of federal tax-exempt income if you use a sell-stop strategy similar to the one proposed in Chapter 7, "High-Yield Bond Funds—Earn the Best Yields Available while Managing the Risks," for corporate high-yield bond funds. Specifically, you need to evaluate the total return of your investment in Nuveen High Yield Municipal Bond Fund at the end of each week. You should sell your shares and move to cash whenever the fund slips by more than 6% from its peak weekly value. Then you stay out of the fund until its total return lifts it at least 6% off of its weekly low point. Using this strategy would have reduced your losses in 2007–2008 from 45% down to below 10%. The reason why I recommend using a 6% sell stop for Nuveen High Yield Municipal Bond Fund instead of the 3% sell stop I recommended for high-yield bond funds in Chapter 7 is that this Nuveen fund has not behaved in exactly the same way as corporate high-yield bond funds.

There is a big caveat with this strategy that you should be aware of. Because there was only one episode when this fund sustained a serious loss, any sell strategy is of necessity constructed to avoid just this one mishap. Normally, when developing a trading strategy, you would like to see how it performed during a number of different episodes to verify that your strategy performs with at least some degree of consistency. With only one major decline to study, we have even less assurance than usual that this sell strategy will protect us the next time this fund suffers a major loss. The reason why it is still worth investing in Nuveen High Yield Municipal Bond Fund (NHMAX) is that a rich experience with corporate high-yield bond funds attests to the success of using sell stops to reduce risk in an analogous but taxable investment. Most important, a 7% tax-free yield is hard to pass up.

# Long-Term Municipal Bonds: You Are Paid to Take the Risk

The data in Table 8–1 show that those mutual funds that hold longer-term bonds pay far better yields than those that hold short-term bonds. For example, the Fidelity Municipal Income Fund (which holds long-term bonds) pays 4.2% per year, whereas the Vanguard Intermediate-Term Tax Exempt Fund pays just 3.4% per year. The downside is that the price risk (interest rate risk) in longer-term bond funds is also much higher—often prohibitively so. As a general rule, I do not recommend buying taxable bonds that mature in more than ten years because the increase in risk beyond that maturity usually outweighs the relatively modest increase in yield. This is especially true for Treasury bonds. On the other hand, municipal bonds pay you better than taxable bonds in return for bearing interest rate risk, making it harder to reject long-term bonds out of hand.

Figure 8–3 shows how interest rates varied for different areas of the bond market, depending on the maturity of the bond. The graphs in Figure 8–3 are called *yield curves*. If you look first at the dashed line, which is the yield curve for investment-grade corporate bonds, you will see at the time this data was collected (4/28/09), 20-year corporates paid an average of 6.7% and 2-year corporates paid 4.6%. The difference between these two yields is 2.1%—it is your additional reward for taking on a great deal of interest rate risk.

Municipal bonds pay you even more for taking on interest rate risk: The 2-year yield was just 0.9% and the 20-year yield was 4.4%. In other words, you received an additional 3.5% for taking on the interest rate risk—a better payoff than the 2.1% you would have gotten from corporate bonds.

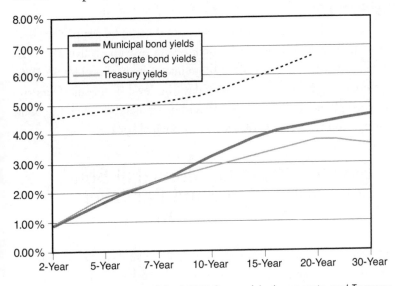

**Figure 8–3**   *Yield curves as of April 2009 for municipal, corporate, and Treasury bonds*

Think about the implications of a 4.4% tax-free yield. On the plus side, you would have to earn 6.8% per year on a taxable investment (if you are in a 35% tax bracket) to match this return. It is not currently possible to earn 6.8% per year without taking some investment risk, whereas the 4.4% per year should be relatively secure if you buy a general obligation bond with a high credit rating. But on the minus side, if inflation averages 3% over the next 20 years, you would be left with just 1.4% of your principal annually to spend, assuming that you wanted to keep up with inflation. Most retirees will need to spend more than just 1.4% of their principal annually.

*The bottom line is that individual long-term municipal bonds can be an attractive source of steady income compared with other bonds if you are in a high tax bracket. However, most retirees will be unable to both keep up with inflation and meet their spending needs over the long term, meaning that you might have to deplete your principal over time as the price of receiving a secure, tax-free income.*

For example, a 20-year municipal bond might be a superior alternative to a fixed annuity for someone who expects to live about 20 more years (i.e., a 66-year-old with no major medical problems). With interest rates as low as they are today, the level of income from the municipal bond and the annuity would be similar, but when the bond matures you would, at least, get your principal back.

# Buying Individual Municipal Bonds— Some Municipal Bond Borrowers Are Safer Than Others

Different municipal bonds have different backing. If you are buying an individual bond, it is important for you to know who is standing behind it. The safest type of municipal bond is called a *general obligation bond*. The borrowing government or entity is a monopoly in its jurisdiction and must use its entire taxing authority to meet its obligations to the bondholders of general obligation bonds. Fitch Ratings conducted large-scale studies of the U.S. municipal bond market from

1987 to 2002. They found that the cumulative default rate for general obligation bonds was just 0.24% during this period.[3] (The cumulative default rate is the total fraction of bonds that defaulted at any point during the period studied.)

Other municipal bonds are backed not by a city or state government generally but rather by the revenues from a particular project. These bonds, called *revenue bonds*, can vary widely in the degree of default risk. Revenue bonds backed by essential government services had a cumulative default rate of 0.70% in the Fitch study, whereas those backed by less-reliable revenue streams (e.g., industrial development bonds, nursing homes) had a cumulative default rate of 3.65%. Moreover, default risks in revenue bonds correlate more strongly with the onset of recession than is the case for general obligation bonds, with defaults generally occurring late in the economic contraction.[4] Given that the United States in 2010 is slowly recovering from a more severe recession than any experienced between 1987 and 2002, default risk in many revenue bonds could be much higher than normal. Under the circumstances, you should confine your individual bond purchases to general obligation bonds unless you have a specific and compelling reason to do otherwise.

# Call Provisions

There are two added twists in buying municipal bonds from a dealer that you are unlikely to face when buying corporates or Treasuries: call provisions and insurance. Before you dive into the municipal bond market, you need to be aware of both issues.

A *callable bond* is one that the borrower can choose to repay before the maturity date. Your mortgage is an example: If interest rates move lower, you can refinance, which basically means paying off your original lender with money you borrowed more cheaply from someone else. The same is true with a callable bond. If you hold one, the borrower can give you back your $1,000/bond before the maturity date. That means that you will have to reinvest the principal at a lower rate than when you initially bought your bond. Note that unlike your mortgage, which you can refinance pretty much at any time, borrowers are more restricted in when they can call bonds from you. Most callable municipal bonds can be called on only a handful of specific dates, although some can be called at any time beyond a particular date.

As a borrower, the ability to call a bond is valuable because you can profit from a drop in interest rates, but you do not bear any risk if interest rates rise. Because the ability to call a bond is favorable to the borrower and potentially risky to the lender, callable bonds generally pay higher interest than noncallable bonds. Of available bonds, municipal bonds are most likely to be callable. If you are far along in retirement and counting on receiving a certain level of interest income, then callable bonds are not for you. On the other hand, if you are confident that you will be able to figure out something productive to do with the proceeds if your bond is called, a callable bond could well be attractive.

Let's look at an example of callable bonds. On 4/28/09, TD Ameritrade listed the general obligation bond shown in Table 8–2.

Table 8-2   *Sample Quotation for a Callable Municipal Bond*

| Issuer | Credit Ratings | Maturity | Coupon | Price | Call Provisions | Yield to Maturity | Yield to Worst Call |
|--------|----------------|----------|--------|-------|-----------------|-------------------|---------------------|
| New York City | Aa3/AA | 9/1/2021 | 5.25% | 110.8 | Any time after 9/1/2018 | 4.123% | 3.86% |

This bond matures in roughly 12.4 years from the date it was offered. During that period, if you bought the bond, you would receive $52.50

in tax-free interest (5.25% of $1,000 par value) each year. However, the quote of 110.8 means that it would have cost $1,108 and not just $1,000 to buy this bond and you will get back just $1,000 when the bond matures or is called—a capital loss of $108. This capital loss offsets some of the interest income, resulting in a yield to maturity of just 4.123%, which is well below the coupon rate of 5.25%.

But it gets worse. If the bond is called as early as possible, which is 9/1/2018, then you will lose the $108 not in 2021, but three years earlier, in 2018. Because the same $108 capital loss would occur over a shorter period of time if the bond is called before it matures, your annual net return between purchasing the bond and having it called will be less than if the bond were not called. The details in the bond offering tell you how much worse: If the bond is called at the worst possible time, your annual return would be 3.86% per year.

*When you are evaluating callable bonds, you need to focus on what your total return will be under the worst-case scenario, which is called the **yield to worst call**, or, for short, the **yield to worst**.* In the case of bonds that are callable within three years or less, the yield to worst is likely to be much worse than the yield to maturity or the coupon rate because interest rates are relatively low by historical standards. You have to take the time to digest all the information in the offering to make sure you know what you are getting paid and to avoid being seduced by the high coupon yields of the past.

# Bond Insurance

Before the financial crisis of 2007–2009, private companies insured the majority of outstanding municipal bonds against default. In case an insured municipal bond did default, the insurance company would pay the bondholders. The price of municipal bond insurance was typically modest, on the order of ¼% per year. By purchasing insurance, a financially mediocre borrower could issue bonds with the top (AAA or Aaa) credit rating of the insurer rather than at their own credit rating.

The problem with municipal bond insurance is that only a handful of firms sell it. That would not pose a problem if a localized catastrophe (like Hurricane Katrina) crippled a small number of issuers. However, the 2007–2009 credit crisis affected almost the entire country at once. That too might be manageable (municipal defaults remain rare as of this writing), except that the same companies that sell municipal bond insurance speculated with their capital in risky ways. As a result, the bond insurance companies became weaker than many of the municipalities they insured, and lost their top credit ratings to boot.

Table 8–3 lists municipal bond insurers that were AAA-rated at the end of 2007, and shows their credit ratings as of April 2009.[5] Of the seven insurers, only two (AGC and FSA) still have credit ratings that make them worthwhile.

Table 8–3    *The Fate of Municipal Bond Insurance Companies That Had Top Credit Ratings at the End of 2007*

| Claims Paying Ability Moody's/S&P/Fitch (as of April 2009) | Insurer |
| --- | --- |
| Ba3/A/na | AMBAC Assurance Corporation |
| Aa2/AAA/AAA | Assured Guaranty Corp. (AGC) |
| Ba3/BB/na | CIFG Assurance North America, Inc. |
| na/CCC/na | Financial Guaranty Insurance Company (FGIC) |
| Aa3/AAA/AAA | Financial Security Assurance Inc. (FSA) |
| Ba1/AA–/na | MBIA Insurance Corp. of Illinois |
| Ca/CC/na | Syncora Guarantee (Formerly XL Capital Assurance ) |

The experiences of the financial markets in 2008–2009 make bond insurance a very dubious benefit, and indeed, the demand for bond insurance by issuers is way down. If you are going to buy an insured bond, try to find out what the uninsured credit rating of the borrower is by looking at their other bonds and use the credit rating of the underlying borrower as a guide. The two bonds shown in Table 8–4, both of which were listed on T.D. Ameritrade's Web site on 4/29/09, show you an example of how to do this. On top is an insured, general obligation bond issued by New York City, and below that is the uninsured New York City general obligation bond we examined earlier.

Table 8–4 *Sample Quotations of an Insured and an Uninsured Municipal Bond from the Same Issuer*

| CUSIP # | Issuer | Ratings | Insurance |
|---------|--------|---------|-----------|
| 64966D-LS-6 | New York City | Aa3/AAA | FSA |
| 64966H-AY-6 | New York City | Aa3/AA | None |

Look at the credit ratings. The top bond, which is insured by FSA, is rated Aa3 by Moody's and AAA by Standard & Poors. (These two ratings disagree with each other in that Standard & Poors has assigned its top rating, while Moody's has assigned a lesser one. However, Standard & Poors has a negative credit watch on FSA, making it quite possible that it will lose its AAA rating.) The uninsured bond is rated Aa3 by Moody's and AA by Standard and Poors. The implication is that if you neglect the bond insurance, a New York City general obligation bond would probably garner an Aa3/AA rating, at least as of this writing. (New York City itself might get downgraded.)

By the way, the left column in the table shows the CUSIP number. As we mentioned in Chapter 2, "Basics of Bond Investments," each publicly traded security (stock, bond, or mutual fund) has its own unique CUSIP number. The CUSIP number does not help you understand the investment, but it should appear on any transaction confirmation that you receive when you buy or sell a bond. Paying attention to the CUSIP number will give you an additional way of making sure you did indeed trade the bond you meant to trade.

# Excellent Source of Municipal Bond Information Online

The Web site, www.investinginbonds.com, is an excellent source of information about the municipal bond market that is independent of any single financial firm. This Web site is maintained by a trade group for the financial industry, the Securities and Financial Markets Association (SIFMA). This Web site contains an overview of the U.S. bond market, allowing you to see at a glance what interest rates different types of bonds are paying. There is also bond market commentary and news, particularly on the municipal bond section of the Web site. But the most interesting feature is the report of daily municipal bond trades.

If you enter the section of the Web site devoted to municipal bonds, you can examine the transactions that have occurred in any particular state or even any particular bond on the current day or historically. This can give you an idea of how much you should be paying for a municipal bond, much like knowing the dealer's invoice price when negotiating to buy a car. (The difference is that wholesale car prices do not usually fluctuate much from one day to the next, whereas bond prices might.) Let's look at an example.

If you had wanted to see the day's transactions in New York State municipal bonds on May 13, 2009, you could have looked into a particular bond, the Hudson Yards Infrastructure Corp. Revenue Series A 5% maturing in 2/15/2047, callable at 100 on 2/15/2007 (shown in Table 8–5). The Web site provides the trading history for each bond, which on this date, included the three transactions shown in Table 8–6.

Table 8–5    *Trade Details for CUSIP: 44420PAC8*

| Ratings | Issuer/CUSIP | State | Coupon/ Maturity | Call Dates | Call Prices | Notes |
|---|---|---|---|---|---|---|
| A (S&P) A3 (Moody's) A- (Fitch) | Hudson Yds Infrastructure Corp NY Rev Series A 44420PAC8 | NY | 5.000 2/15/2047 | 2/15/2007 | 100 | Nontaxable Book entry only |

Table 8–6    *All Transactions in a Particular Municipal Bond (CUSIP 44420PAC8) on 5/13/2009*

| Trade Date/ Trade Time | Price | Yield (to Worst) | Size | Trade Type | More Info. |
|---|---|---|---|---|---|
| 5/13/2009 13:04:18 | 96.000 | 5.244 | 50K | Sale to customer | Run calculations |
| 5/13/2009 13:00:16 | 93.25 | | 50K | Interdealer | Run calculations |
| 5/13/2009 12:38:59 | 92.000 | 5.505 | 50K | Purchase from customer | Run calculations |

Three transactions in this bond, all the same size, are listed from most recent to earliest. These three transactions occurred within a half hour on a day when the municipal bond market was quiet. A customer sold 50 bonds (par value $50,000, abbreviated as 50K on the Web site) for 92 (i.e., $920) each to a broker/dealer. Shortly thereafter, a different broker found a customer to whom he sold the same bonds at a price of 96 ($960), which is 4.3% higher than the other customer received. A middleman paid 93.25 for the bonds four minutes before they were sold at 96 to the customer.

The inference is that a broker lined up a customer to buy these 50 bonds at 96, knowing that he could buy them for 93.25. Once the customer agreed to buy at 96, the broker bought the bonds from another broker/dealer at 93.25 and four minutes later put the bonds into his customer's account for 96, making a profit of 2.75 per bond. This represented a markup of almost 3% from his cost. The broker's dollar profit on this 50-bond trade was $1,375, some of which went to the broker himself and some to his firm. The interdealer price was 93.25, which represents the true "wholesale" price for this bond at that time.

The only drawback about using this type of data is that only completed transactions are posted. In the preceding example, the customer would not have known the size of his broker's markup until after completing the transaction. One possibility is to place a trial order with a broker (for an individual municipal bond) and check later in the day to see if the broker bought the bonds from a dealer. However, if you use a broker from a firm that is itself a bond dealer, you still might not gather information about how much of a profit the broker made. Even though this Web site falls short of the type of full disclosure you can get for stock quotations, you still might be able to arm yourself with enough information to knock a percent or so off of the price that your broker is quoting you for municipal bonds.

One last point about the information on this Web site: If you click the Run Calculations link, a new screen appears that contains the yield to maturity, the yield to each call date, and the yield to worst, along with the schedule of all expected interest and principal payments during the remaining life of the bond.

# Conclusion

Municipal bonds are great if you want to minimize your tax bill. The best way to invest in short-term municipal bonds (those that mature in three years or less) is with one of the several municipal bond funds recommended in this chapter. On the other hand, if you want to invest for more than ten years, if you have sufficient capital (at least $25,000) to diversify, and if you have a broker you trust, individual municipal bonds are likely to be best for you. In addition to buying investment-grade municipal bonds, I recommend the Nuveen High Yield Municipal Bond Fund (NHMAX) as a potentially more speculative but higher-yielding investment. As always, you should buy this fund only through a discount broker such as Schwab or T.D. Ameritrade without paying a sales load.

# chapter 9

# Preferred Stocks—Obtain Higher Yields Than You Can with Corporate Bonds

There is a little-known corner of the stock market where you can garner above-average dividend yields, and maybe some tax advantage to boot: preferred stocks. Preferred stocks in solid companies are currently paying 6%–7% in dividend income—some 1%–2% per year more than the interest you could get from bonds in similar companies. Unfortunately, you don't get this extra yield for free: Preferred stocks are not as safe as bonds. The events of 2008 serve as a warning that you have to be very careful about how you utilize these types of investments. This chapter shows you how.

## Features of Preferred Stocks

Preferred stocks trade on stock exchanges the same as common stocks and exchange-traded funds (ETFs), which is to say that you buy and sell them through a broker. Unlike common stocks, which represent a share of the entire company, preferred stocks are loans that pay interest to you, the shareholder. In many ways, preferred stocks are more like bonds than like common stocks.

We have already seen that when a company issues bonds to borrow money, it specifies the dollar amount of interest it will pay each year. Preferred stocks share the same attributes: Each is issued with a preset dividend payment schedule. For example, a company might issue a preferred stock at $25/share that pays $1.50/year in dividends. That translates into a yield of 6.0%.

Bonds all have maturity dates when the original principal of the loan will be repaid. Many preferred stocks have maturity dates as well, although as a rule they are at least 30 years after issuance. Many other preferred stocks are perpetual—the principal is never repaid, so the shareholder collects interest forever (or at least until he sells the shares to someone else).

Unlike most corporate bonds, preferred stocks are callable. This means that whenever the cost of borrowing drops below the dividend that the preferred stock is paying, the issuer can redeem your shares and repay you the principal amount, which is usually $25/share. With many callable bonds, the issuer can call on at most a small number of days specified at the time the bond is issued. In contrast, preferred stocks can be called at any time after 5 years of being issued. In this regard, preferred stocks are like your 30-year mortgage: You can refinance whenever interest rates move in your favor, but you can also choose to keep making payments for 30 years.

# Taxes on Preferred Stock Dividends

From the tax perspective, there are two types of preferred stocks: those whose dividends are taxed the same way as bond interest and those whose dividends are taxed the same as qualified common stock dividends. Because the taxes on qualified dividends are currently much lower than the taxes on bond interest, you should seek out preferred stocks that receive the better tax treatment for a taxable investment account. (The Web site I recommend later in the "How to Find Information about Preferred Stocks" section, www.quantumonline. com, provides this information.) However, the current tax break accorded to qualified dividends is scheduled to expire after 2010, so before you make any tax-motivated investment decisions, you need to make sure you understand any changes in how dividends are taxed. Remember, if you are buying preferred stocks for an IRA, there is no tax advantage to qualified dividends. In that case, you should seek out the highest yield available from a safe investment, regardless of its tax treatment.

# Price Risk with Preferred Stocks

Preferred stock prices depend on three factors: the creditworthiness of the borrower, the attractiveness of the dividend, and the call provisions.

The first factor, the creditworthiness of the borrower, is self-explanatory. If the company that issued the preferred stock is in trouble, investors recognize the significant risk that preferred and common shareholders will be wiped out, so the price of the preferred stock drops to reflect that risk. If you buy a preferred stock in a troubled company (likely for a discount from its original issue price) and the situation improves, the price of your stock will rise.

The preferred issue from AT&T (ticker symbol ATT, not to be confused with the common stock, whose ticker symbol is T) provides an example of the level of price volatility you could see during turbulent market periods. Figure 9–1 shows two years' total returns (2007–2009) for both the common and preferred stock issues of AT&T. During the period shown, the preferred stock gained 18% with a worst drawdown of 21%, whereas the common stock lost 22% and had a worst drawdown of 46%. Clearly, the preferred stock was less risky (and in this case, also more profitable) than the common stock. However, the preferred stock was no walk in the park. Even though the episodic declines in the preferred stock did ultimately reverse themselves in relatively short order, this level of volatility would have been very scary to a safety-conscious investor.

Stock and bond market volatility in 2008 was extremely high by historical standards. I am hopeful (but cannot guarantee, of course) that the preferred stock of AT&T will give a quieter ride in the years to come. ATT currently yields 6.3% and is rated A3/A (Moody's/Standard & Poors), which is about average for investment-grade corporate debt and which is a solid credit rating. As of November 2009, the credit rating outlook for AT&T is stable. Its preferred stock dividends are taxed at the same (higher) rate as bond interest.

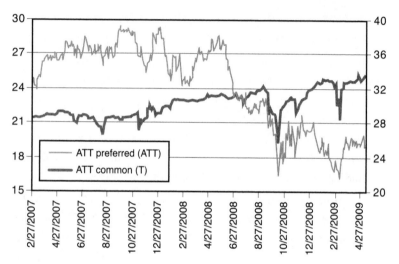

**Figure 9-1** *Performance (including dividends) of one share of the common and preferred stock issues for AT&T, 2007-2009*

The second factor, which also applies to bonds, is how the dividend payout compares with prevailing interest rates. If preferred stock XYZ issued at $25 is paying $1.50 (6%), but newly issued preferred stocks are paying $1.75 (7% of $25), the price of XYZ will be lower than its issue price. This is the same for bonds: If interest rates rise after a bond is issued, the market price of previously issued bonds falls.

Call provisions are the trickiest to address quantitatively. We have already seen that when preferred stock yields rise, the prices of existing preferred stocks fall. However, the converse might not be true: A drop in interest rates might not boost shares of preferred stocks *if the issuer can call the shares.*

The analogy to a mortgage is again helpful. If interest rates rise, you will not refinance your mortgage, but if interest rates fall, then you might. Similarly, if interest rates fall, your preferred shares will not be worth more than the issue price of $25 (for example) because the company can force you to turn over your shares for $25 whenever it is in the issuer's benefit to do so. The only way that preferred shares can rise above $25 when interest rates drop is if the shares are not callable.

So like a mortgage lender, as a preferred shareholder, you can only lose when interest rates change. If interest rates rise, your shares lose value, but if interest rates fall, you do not get the benefits. For this reason, preferred stock dividends have to be high enough to compensate the shareholder's asymmetric exposure to the risks of interest rate changes.

Knowing that preferred stocks can be called, I do not recommend ever paying more than the par value for a share of preferred stock if the share is callable. If you buy a share of preferred stock that is at a big discount to its issue price because interest rates have since gone up, you will be in a position to profit if interest rates drop.

# Credit Risk with Preferred Stocks

Like bonds, if a company defaults on its debt, the preferred shareholders will stop receiving dividends and will basically lose the entire value of their investments. In fact, when companies default on their bond debt, bondholders have on average received about 50 cents on the dollar. Preferred shareholders have not been that lucky because they stand in line behind bondholders when it comes to dividing up the remnants of a failed company. When a company defaults on its debt, preferred shareholders are generally wiped out along with common shareholders. This is what befell preferred shareholders in the government-sponsored mortgage giants, Fannie Mae and Freddie Mac in 2008, even though investors in these entities' bonds received a federal guarantee and, therefore, did not lose anything. When Lehman Brothers went bankrupt in September 2008, all its creditors were sunk. Bondholders received about 10 cents on the dollar, while common and preferred shareholders were left with nothing.

The reason for the name "preferred" is that preferred shareholders get their dividends before common shareholders do in the event that the company does not have enough cash to pay both. A company can cut its common stock dividend to conserve cash, but it cannot adjust its preferred dividend. All it can do is pay up or default.

Many preferred stocks are **noncumulative**. This means that if a company cannot pay a scheduled preferred dividend, it can skip the payment and not have to make up for it later. In this regard, the noncumulative preferred stock issuer gets a better deal than you do with your mortgage. The only guarantee that preferred shareholders have of receiving dividends is that before common shareholders get any payout at all, the preferred shareholders must first receive their scheduled dividend payments.

Cumulative preferred stock is a better deal than noncumulative: If a company misses a dividend payment to preferred shareholders, it must make up for it later before paying anything to common shareholders. Either way, preferred shareholders are behind bondholders in terms of getting paid in the event that a company cannot meet its debt obligations.

# Watching Your Sector Exposure

The vast majority of preferred stocks are issued by financial companies. This means that if you buy a representative cross section of the preferred stock universe, you will be highly exposed to the risk in that sector. As of late 2009, banks have passed their government-mandated stress tests, and things are looking brighter for the financial sector. Nonetheless, there is always the possibility that banks' exposures to commercial real estate will cause them to stumble again, even as they are recovering from their exposure to residential mortgages.

There are ETFs that own baskets of preferred stocks, such as the iShares S&P U.S. Preferred Stock Index ETF (PFF). This ETF is 83% in financial stocks, and as a result, has risen and fallen in tandem with the changing fortunes of the sector. Figure 9–2 shows this, comparing the price behavior of PFF and that of the Financial Sector SPDR (XLF) in 2007–2009. Notice that both the Financial Sector SPDR and the preferred stock ETF hit major low points simultaneously, for example on 3/17/2008, 7/15/2008, 11/20/2008, and 3/9/2009.

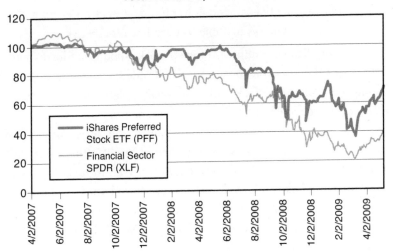

**Total Returns, 2007-2009**

**Figure 9–2** *iShares U.S. Preferred Stock ETF (PFF) and the Financial Sector SPDR (XLF), 2007–2009*

Avoiding financial issues of preferred stocks is like combing through the bargain rack in search of the perfect article of clothing. You can often find what you like, but it takes a lot of work to screen out what you don't like. I have done much of the work for you here.

Table 9–1 was originally published in my investment newsletter "Systems and Forecasts" (www.systemsandforecasts.com) in 2008, and is updated here. The stocks in Table 9–1 have been selected from over 600 listed on Quantum Online whose dividends are taxed at the more favorable rate. This list is further narrowed by considering only preferred stocks that have investment-grade credit ratings, are in non-financial companies, and are traded on the New York Stock Exchange (NYSE) or the American Stock Exchange (AMEX). Most of the stocks that meet these criteria are utility stocks. (The current yields and ticker symbols for the stocks in Table 9–1 came from www.nyse.com or www.amex.com. Note that the NYSE and AMEX originated as separate exchanges. They have since merged but still maintain different systems of assigning ticker symbols to preferred stocks. Except where noted, the ticker symbols in Table 9–1 are from the NYSE.)

The abundance of utility preferred stocks should not lead you to overweight them in your own portfolio. Prudence suggests that you should diversify, especially with potentially volatile investments. If utility preferred stocks remain attractive at the time you are considering making an investment, choose companies from different areas of the country, preferably those with a current credit rating of at least Baa/BBB. Ideally, you should also check the Web to make sure that the company whose preferred stock you are considering is not on negative credit watch. Of the utilities in Table 9–1, the only one on negative credit watch as of November 2009 was XCEL Energy, but that could change at any time.

There is one other caveat you should note about the preferred stocks in Table 9–1. Some, such as DuPont or Consolidated Edison (New York City's electric utility), have common stocks that give you close to the same dividend yield as the preferred. If that is the case, it means that the common stock is relatively cheap and that you should investigate further before making a decision. It could turn out that the common stock is the more attractive income-generating investment. In the case of DuPont (DD), the company is on negative credit watch as of November 2009, so you should probably hold off on buying that preferred issue until the credit outlook becomes stable.

Some closed-end mutual funds issue preferred stock to borrow money that they use to leverage their portfolios. These types of preferred stocks are attractive because they are backed by relatively liquid investment collateral in the form of individual stocks held in the funds' portfolios. The value of the investments in the closed-end funds would have to fall by 70% or more before a fund's assets became inadequate to cover the debt owed to the preferred shareholders. That is why they have triple-A ratings. The stocks listed in Table 9–1 are a good place to start in your search for preferred stocks. I especially like the shares issued by closed-end mutual funds (Gabelli Funds, Royce Funds), in addition to the issue from AT&T (ATT) mentioned previously. You can also consider new preferred stock issues that meet the same criteria as they come out.

**Table 9–1**  *Preferred Stocks Whose Dividends Qualify for More Favorable Tax Treatment*

| Ticker Symbol NYSE.com | Company Name | Yield (%) | Credit Ratings (Moody's/S&P) |
|---|---|---|---|
| | **Mutual Fund Preferred Stocks** | | |
| GCVPRB | Gabelli Convertible and Income Securities Fund | 6.1% | Aaa |
| GGNPRA | Gabelli Global Gold Natural Resources and Income | 6.5% | Aaa |

Table 9-1 *Continued*

| Ticker Symbol NYSE.com | Series Letters | Company Name | Yield (%) | Credit Ratings (Moody's/S&P) |
|---|---|---|---|---|
| GDVPRA | | Gabelli Dividend and Income Trust | 6.1% | Aaa |
| GDVPRD | | Gabelli Dividend and Income Trust | 6.0% | Aaa |
| GABPRF | | Gabelli Equity Trust | 6.1% | Aaa/AAA |
| | | **Mutual Fund Preferred Stocks** | | |
| GABPRD | | Gabelli Equity Trust | 6.0% | Aaa/AAA |
| GGTPRB | | Gabelli Global Multimedia Trust | 6.1% | Aaa/not rated |
| GUTPRA | | Gabelli Utility Trust | 5.3% | Aaa/AAA |
| RFOPRA | | Royce Focus Trust | 6.0% | Aaa/no rating |
| RMTPRA | | Royce Micro-Cap Trust | 6.1% | Aaa/no rating |
| RVTPRB | | Royce Value Trust | 6.1% | Aaa/no rating |
| | Series Letters | **Nonutility Industrial Company** | | |
| DDPRA | A,B | DuPont | 5.4% | A2/BBB+ |
| | Series Letters | **Utility Preferred Stocks** | | |
| ALPPRP | N,O,P | Alabama Power | 5.6% | Baa1/BBB+ |
| ABA | JJ | Alabama Power | 6.10% | Baa1/BBB+ |
| EDPRA | A | Consolidated Edison | 5.6% | A3/BBB |
| EDPRC | C | Consolidated Edison | 5.8% | A3/BBB |
| GPEPRA | A | Georgia Power Co. | 6.1% | Baa1/BBB+ |
| IPLPRC | | Interstate Power and Light | 7.0% | Baa2/BBB- |
| IPLPRB | | Interstate Power and Light | 7.5% | Baa2/BBB- |
| MPPRD | | Mississippi Power Co. | 5.3% | A3/BBB+ |

| Ticker Symbol NYSE.com | | Company Name | Yield (%) | Credit Ratings (Moody's/S&P) |
|---|---|---|---|---|
| NMKPRC | B,C | Niagara Mohawk Power Corp | 5.0% | Baa2/BBB |
| NMKPRB | | Niagara Mohawk Power Corp | 4.6% | Baa2/BBB |
| PGC.PR.E | C,D,E,G,H,I | Pacific Gas and Electric (AMEX) | 5.9% | Baa2/BBB– |
| PPW.PR | | Pacificorp (AMEX) | 6.0% | Baa3/BBB |
| PPLPRB | A,B | PPL Electric Utility Corp. | 5.6% | Baa3/BBB |
| SDO.PR.H | A,B,C,H | San Diego Gas and Electric (AMEX) | 6.7% | Baa1/BBB+ |
| SGCPR | | South Carolina Electric and Gas Co. | 4.8% | Baa2/BBB |
| SCE.PR.E | B,C,D,E | Southern California Edison (AMEX) | 6.0% | Baa2/BBB– |
| VELPRE | | Virginia Electric and Power | 5.4% | Baa3/BBB |
| WIS.PR | | Wisconsin Power and Light (AMEX) | 5.3% | Baa1/BBB |
| XELPRG | A,B,C,D,E,G | Xcel Energy | 5.7% | Baa3/BBB– |

Even though I recommend the preferred stocks in Table 9–1 that are from closed-end mutual funds, you should keep in mind that their prices can be volatile, especially in the face of a steep stock market decline that threatens the value of the funds' ability to repay preferred stockholders. Buy the stocks only below their par value of $25/share. As another example of how volatile preferred stocks can be, Figure 9–3 shows the history of the Royce Focus Trust Preferred A (RFO-PRA) from 2004 to 2009. This stock has mostly stayed within a range of $22 to $26/share, but as with most preferred stocks, this one took a dive during the fourth quarter of 2008. The Royce Focus Trust Preferred A got as low as $17 but has since recovered much of its value, showing it to be significantly less volatile than iShares U.S. Preferred Stock ETF (PFF). The dividend payout for Royce Focus Trust Preferred A is $1.50/year, which at the current share price of $23.38 is 6.4% per year. This issue is callable at any time.

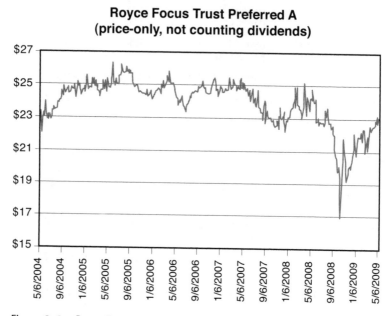

**Royce Focus Trust Preferred A**
**(price-only, not counting dividends)**

Figure 9–3    *Royce Focus Trust Preferred A, 2004–2009*

# How to Find Information about Preferred Stocks

Researching preferred stocks is very cumbersome. For one thing, there is not even a uniform system of ticker symbols. That means that the symbol you enter to get information on www.nyse.com could well be different from what you would enter to get information about the same stock on Yahoo! Finance. In fact, even within www.nyse.com

there are inconsistencies. Preferred stocks that used to trade on the American Stock Exchange but which are now listed on the New York Stock Exchange (NYSE) have a different system of symbols than preferred stocks that have been listed on the NYSE from their issue. Even though there are different systems of symbols, it is usually pretty straightforward to recognize when two different symbols represent the same preferred stock.

Another problem for the preferred stock investor is that financial Web sites such as Yahoo! Finance or MSN Investor that are so helpful for ETFs and for common stocks frequently do not provide data on listed preferred stocks. I have found two valuable online resources for preferred stocks:

- www.quantumonline.com
- www.nyse.com

Quantum Online offers descriptions of each preferred issue, including dividend amount, credit ratings, call dates, maturity dates, and links to the prospectus. The NYSE Web site gives you ready access to the most recent price and dividend yield for listed preferred stocks.

# Trading Preferred Stocks

Preferred stocks are more difficult to trade than common stocks or ETFs for a number of reasons. First, there is very little trading activity in preferred stocks. Some preferred issues might not trade at all on any given day. When stocks are infrequently traded, or traded in just small amounts, they are said to be illiquid. When you buy an illiquid stock, you are at risk for overpaying by a percent or so, and when you sell an illiquid stock, you are at risk for receiving too little. To get an idea of how fairly you will be treated, you should know the bid price and the ask price for the preferred stock you want. If the spread (difference) between the bid and ask prices is less than ½% of the bid price, you can have a high degree of confidence that the cost of buying and selling the stock will be reasonable.

Because so many preferred stocks are illiquid, you should make sure you are in love with a stock before you buy it because you should plan on holding it for years. The amount of dividend income has to be attractive enough to make that kind of mental commitment. Of course, if your situation or the situation of the underlying company changes, you are free to sell your preferred shares. Just understand that the decision to sell could cost you 1% of your investment or even more.

# Where Do Preferred Stocks Fit into Your Portfolio?

Because of the trading costs and price risks, you should not overinvest in preferred stocks. As with individual corporate bonds, no more than 1%–2% of your total portfolio should be invested with any one issuing company. I would limit preferred stocks to 10% of your total income-producing portfolio. That way, if preferreds suffer a 20% price decline, your loss will be a manageable 1%–2% of total assets, which you can ride out while continuing to collect the interest.

You should only buy a preferred stock if you are satisfied with the level of its dividend and would be willing to collect it for years to come. Because inflation has averaged more than 4% per year since the end of World War II, you should not buy a preferred stock that pays less than 6% per year. Only that level of interest will give you enough cushion against the possibility that inflation will rise again, even though consumer prices rose just 0.1% in 2008. Under current market and economic conditions, I recommend the preferred stocks from the Royce and Gabelli funds and the preferred issue from AT&T if you can buy them below the stocks' par value.

You should not buy preferred stocks in search of capital gains due to interest rate changes or improvements in credit ratings because of the magnitude of the trading costs (bid/ask spread) for preferred stocks. If you want to position yourself for an improvement in the financial condition of an individual company, the common stock will probably serve you best. If you want to position yourself for changes in interest rates, a diversified bond investment will meet that need.

# Other Types of Preferred Stocks

We have been discussing only traditional preferred stocks. There are other types of investments also called preferred stocks that I do not recommend, so make sure you know what you are buying.

It is very common for brokers to package what are basically bonds in the form of what appear to be preferred stocks. Such bonds in disguise are called trust preferred stocks. There is nothing wrong with that. In fact, you might have better protection in the event of a default with a trust preferred stock than with a traditional preferred stock because you might be in the same group with the other bondholders. The drawback with trust preferred stocks is that their dividends do not receive the advantageous tax treatment accorded to qualified dividends. Rather, trust preferred stock dividends are subject to the more onerous ordinary income tax rates that apply to other taxable corporate bond interest payments.

In addition, a number of convertible preferred stocks are available. The preferred shareholder can exchange (convert) each share of preferred stock for a number of shares of the common stock that is fixed at the time the preferred stock is issued. Typically, when a convertible preferred stock is issued, the price of the common stock is below where it would make sense to convert the preferred shares. Rather, if you hold a newly issued convertible preferred, you will likely opt to collect interest. But if the common stock appreciates sufficiently, the value of the convertible preferred shares will be determined not by the dividends paid but by the value of the common shares for which the preferred share can be exchanged. At that point, the common and preferred shares will move in parallel, and the interest you receive from the preferred shares will likely be lower than what you could get from traditional preferred stocks. If you like the dividend rate and the underlying company, buying a recently issued convertible preferred stock might make sense.

A vehicle called auction rate preferred stocks achieved notoriety in 2008. Unlike traditional preferred stocks, auction rate preferreds generally sell for $25,000/share and were, therefore, marketed to institutions and wealthy investors. The theory was that borrowers would issue preferreds that would mature in 30 years. However, the interest rate was not fixed at the time of issue as it would be with a traditional preferred stock. Rather, the rate would be determined weekly at auction: Whichever investor was willing to accept the lowest rate for the week got the stock. In this way, the borrower could pay only short-term interest rates because the rates were reset each week. The investor had the confidence that whenever he wanted to cash out, there would always be someone else willing to take his shares off of his hands. Auction rate preferreds were touted as alternatives to the money market for cash reserves because the interest they paid was slightly higher.

Problems began when some of the borrowers appeared to be in trouble, along with a host of other credit fears in 2008. Once investors became fearful, they stopped bidding for auction rate preferreds. Shareholders who had expected to be able to get out with just a week's notice were stuck with 30-year preferred stocks for the first time.

Auction rate preferred stocks did have a contingency clause that in the event that the shares could not be sold at auction due to lack of interest (a "failed auction"), the interest rate would revert to one calculated by a predetermined formula. Some of these auction rate preferred stocks were issued by municipal governments, and these tended to have very generous yields in the event of failed auctions. In this case, the issuers were on the short end of the stick because their interest cost went up unexpectedly. They borrowed money from the municipal bond market with which to repurchase their auction rate preferreds so that their interest costs were again in line with market levels.

Other issuers simply had to pay a short-term rate based on market yields, which means that the shareholders were stuck with an illiquid 30-year bond paying only money market rates. Some big institutions such as UBS were forced by regulatory authorities to repurchase now-unwanted auction rate securities from their customers who were not adequately apprised of their risks. Needless to say, nobody is trying to sell new auction rate issues right now because the meager rewards do not justify taking on the big risks.

# Conclusion

Preferred stocks offer potentially attractive yields for the investor who is willing to tolerate some volatility in the share prices. Investors who are seeking attractive levels of interest income can invest up to 10% of their portfolio in a variety of preferred stocks, but should not place more than 1%–2% of their assets in any single company. Particular preferred stock issues that I recommend are those from AT&T (ATT) and those issued by the Gabelli and Royce mutual funds. But remember, do not buy any preferred stock above the price at which it could be called.

Most preferred stocks are issued by financial companies. Fortunately, as of late 2009, the financial sector appears to have stabilized. This means that income-seeking investors can cautiously take on some exposure to the sector. Preferred stock ETFs such as iShares

S&P U.S. Preferred Stock Index ETF (PFF) or the PowerShares Preferred Stock ETF (PGX) will be the easiest way to participate in this type of investment. How will you recognize when financial companies are again in danger? That is a question on everyone's mind, and there is no easy answer. To mitigate the risk of too much exposure to the financial sector, you should make the effort to place half of your preferred stock investments in other sectors such as the ones recommended earlier in this chapter.

# chapter 10

# Why Even Conservative Investors Need Some Exposure to Other Markets

We have seen that bond investments have usually been safe, but that during periods of economic upheaval, even bonds can be riskier than you might desire. Wouldn't it be great if there were another type of investment that you could add to your bond portfolio that would decrease its risk without hurting (and maybe even helping) returns?

There is such an investment—stocks. Adding some stocks to your bond portfolio would historically have made it safer, even though stocks by themselves have been far riskier than bonds. In this chapter, you will see why this has been the case and how much of your conservative investment portfolio you should allocate to stocks.

## The Bond Market Likes Recessions and Hates Expansions

Recessions are periods when the economy is shrinking. That means fewer people are buying things, and businesses are investing less in new factories, equipment, and so on. With less demand for everything, prices are less likely to increase and, in many cases, might fall. Just as the demand for goods and services falls during recessions, so too does the demand for credit. That allows interest rates to fall, increasing the prices of existing bonds.

So bondholders win two ways during recessions: The prices of their bonds increase and inflation decreases. (However, investors in high-yield bond funds do not revel in bad economic news because for potentially shaky companies, the increased risk of default during recessions outweighs the benefit of falling interest rates.)

The problem for bondholders occurs during the recovery, which reverses the conditions that were favorable for them (and painful for everyone else). If you were fortunate enough to have bought bonds before the threat of recession loomed, you can hold them through the recession and recovery, likely ending up more or less where you started in terms of bond prices, but having enjoyed several years of interest payments. However, if you are unlucky enough to buy bonds in the middle of a recession, you are likely to lose money during the subsequent recovery.

Recessions are relatively infrequent, but unfortunately, bondholders face price risks even in the absence of a full-blown recession. Anytime that investors collectively fear deflation—periods of overall falling prices—bondholders will profit. But when that fear abates, bondholders will give back their deflation-inspired gains. If you buy bonds in the middle of a deflation scare, you are locking in unfavorable interest rates and are setting yourself up for losses when price pressures revert to their normal, mildly inflationary state.

# The Stock Market Likes Expansions and Hates Recessions

For all the reasons that investment-grade bondholders like recessions, stock investors dislike them. Anyone who owns or works for a business knows that the decline in demand during recessions reduces sales and hurts profits. Recession (or the threat of one) is bad for stock prices.

The bottom line is that if you happen to own both stocks and bonds, there is a good chance that owning stocks could cancel out some of your risk from bonds during periods when economic growth is expected, and that owning bonds could cancel out some of your stock market risk during periods when economic deceleration or outright contraction is expected. *To the extent that stocks cancel out the risk from bonds and vice versa, you have the potential to be safer holding both stocks and bonds than you would if you held either one exclusively.*

Let's see how that would have worked out historically. Table 10–1 shows the average compounded annual gains and worst drawdowns for stocks, bonds, and different combinations of the two. (Stocks are represented by the S&P 500 Index including dividends, and bonds are represented by the Barclay's Capital U.S. Aggregate Bond Index including interest. Data are monthly, starting 12/31/1975 through 2/28/2009.)

Table 10–1    *Long-Term Results from Investing in Different Combinations of Stocks and Bonds*

| Portfolio Composition | Compounded Annual Gain 1976–2008 | Worst Drawdown |
|---|---|---|
| 100% bonds | 8.4% | -13% |
| 75% bonds/25% stocks | 8.9% | -12% |
| 50% bonds/50% stocks | 9.4% | -27% |
| 25% bonds/75% stocks | 9.8% | -40% |
| 100% stocks | 9.9% | -51% |

Notice that the portfolio that was 75% in bonds and 25% in stocks was slightly *safer* than the all-bond portfolio (drawdown of -12% for the diversified portfolio versus -13% for the all-bond portfolio). It also returned a bit more (8.9% per year versus 8.4% per year).

In the past ten years, bond returns have been highest when the stock market has performed badly, and vice versa. Figure 10–1 shows the performance of investments in the S&P 500 Index and in long-term U.S. Treasury bonds (as represented by the Vanguard

Long-Term U.S. Treasury Bond Fund, VUSTX). During those years in the past decade when stocks did poorly overall (2000–2002, 2007–2009), Treasuries were very strong. When the stock market was strong (2002–2007), Treasuries were weak.

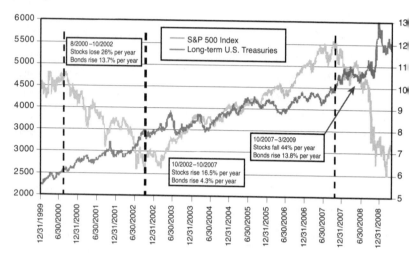

Figure 10–1    *Growth of investments in long-term Treasuries and in the S&P 500 Index (total returns, 2000–2009)*

There is another reason besides just diversification to include some stocks in even a conservative portfolio. The 2000–2009 period was the worst for stocks since the Great Depression. Although nothing is guaranteed, history does suggest that the coming decade (or two) will be better for stocks than the last one. There is no similar assurance that investment-grade bonds will perform better from 2010–2020 than they did from 2000–2009 (5.7% per year) because interest rates are lower now than they were in 2000.

You should also note that stocks and bonds have not always balanced each other out the way they have from 1999–2009. During the 1970s and early 1980s, the economy experienced both a recession and high inflation (with resultant rising interest rates). That was bad for both stocks and bonds. There were a number of factors responsible for this period of *stagflation*, including soaring commodity prices. If we suffer another era of stagflation, bonds and stocks will probably not effectively diversify each other. During a period of stagflation, cash is king.

# Conclusion

As of late 2009, the recommended portfolio for conservative, income-seeking investors is to be 75% in diverse bond investments and 25% in equities. Your investment-grade taxable bond investments should lean toward the shorter term or should utilize active strategies such as the use of buy stops and sell stops to trade high-yield bond funds. The next two chapters describe equity strategies that you can use for that portion of your investments to participate in the potential growth of the stock market over the long term but with a measure of protection against the risks.

chapter 11

# Equity ETFs for Dividend Income

In the previous chapter, we saw that historically, even conservative investors would have benefited by having up to 25% of their portfolio in equities. In this chapter and the two that follow, you see how to select stock market investments that are likely (but, unfortunately, not guaranteed) to be safer than the overall stock market with no reduction in potential returns. These investments will involve buying ETFs or mutual funds, which you can accomplish without being an expert at picking stocks and at a minimum of effort.

## The Importance of Dividends

There are two sources of potential profit from owning stocks: capital gains and dividend income. Capital gains represent an increase in the price of your shares, which can be significant over a period of several years or more. Dividends are cash payments that most companies make to their shareholders, and these too can be significant over the long term. Unlike preferred stock dividends, which cannot be modified, companies can raise or lower their common stock dividends at will. Traditionally, companies have been hesitant to reduce dividends, even in the face of a short-term earnings shortfall, because that would signal longer-term pessimism to the marketplace, potentially depressing the share price.

Usually, profits from a company's operations provide the cash with which to pay dividends. However, at times, a company might choose to deplete its own cash reserves or even borrow in the bond market to raise the cash to maintain a common stock dividend if the company's directors believe that the company retains the capacity to earn more than its dividend over the long term. For example, as of data reported on Yahoo! Finance on 5/14/09, DuPont (DD) was earning just $1.42/share while continuing to pay a common stock dividend of $1.68/share. Clearly, DuPont management expected earnings to increase sufficiently to cover the dividend at this level because if they did not, they would have reduced the dividend payout. Based on third quarter 2009 financial results, it appears that management's optimism was justified. In 2008–2009, companies such as General Electric (GE) that previously had solid records of maintaining or growing dividends bit the bullet and cut their payouts because of an acute need for cash to cover losses related to their exposure to mortgages and other consumer debt.

Since the 1980s, companies have returned cash to their shareholders by buying back shares on the open market in addition to paying dividends. There are a number of reasons for this:

- Capital gains far exceeded dividend payouts in the 1980s and 1990s, leading investors to downplay the importance of dividends in their collective psyches.

- The payment of stock options to company employees dilutes the value of outstanding shares because, in essence, the company is creating shares to use to pay salaries and bonuses. Buying back shares cancels out the dilutional effects of issuing stock options.

- Before 2003, dividends were taxed doubly and heavily: The corporation had to pay income taxes and then the shareholder receiving the dividend had to pay ordinary income rates too. In that situation, company cash used to buy back shares would result (theoretically) in a superior after-tax return to the shareholders than the same amount of cash paid out as dividends. Now, however, shareholders generally pay the lower long-term capital gains tax rate on dividends. (See the sidebar "Taxation of Stock Dividends.") It remains to be seen how dividends will be treated in the years ahead when the tax code is modified.

## TAXATION OF STOCK DIVIDENDS

Common or preferred stock dividends called *qualified dividends* are subject to the same federal income tax as long-term capital gains, on which the maximum federal rate is 15% (as of late 2009). There are some caveats, however. First, you have to own the common shares that paid the dividend for more than 60 days. If a preferred stock pays a qualified dividend, you have to have held it for more than 90 days to get the favored tax treatment. (See IRS Publication 550, "Investment Income and Expenses," available online at www.irs.gov.)

Second, dividends from companies that do not pay corporate income tax (such as real estate investment trusts) or that can deduct the dividend from their own taxable income (some preferred stock dividends) are taxed the same as ordinary income, with a maximum federal tax rate of 35% as of late 2009.

According to the definitive long-term stock market data compiled by Ibbotson,[1] the total return from large U.S. company stocks from the end of 1925 through the end of 2007 averaged 10.4% per year (compounded annually). Of this 10.4% per year, 6.0% per year arose from capital gains and 4.2% per year from dividends. However, as of late 2009, the dividend yield on large-company U.S. stocks is just 2.0%, significantly below the long-term average of 4.2%. That makes it somewhat difficult to find stock investments with dividend yields comparable to bond yields.

As a rule of thumb, when the dividend yield on the S&P 500 Index reaches 3%, you can consider the stock market to be fairly valued by historical standards of the past 50 years. That does not guarantee that stocks will only go higher once dividends reach 3%, but does suggest the potential for historically average returns going forward over the long term.[2]

There are two potential advantages to you in seeking above-average dividend yields from a diversified equity investment:

- Dividend income is currently taxed at a less onerous rate than taxable bond interest.

- Research has found that stocks with above-average yields have collectively outperformed the overall stock market.

Let's look at two long-term studies on the advantages of stocks with above-average dividends. The first is in James O'Shaughnessy's *What Works On Wall Street, 3rd Edition* (McGraw-Hill, 2005). He studied all large company U.S. stocks compared with the 50 with the highest-dividend yield (evaluated once each year). During 1952–2003, large company stocks returned an average of 11.7% per year (compounded, including reinvestment of dividends), versus 13.6% per year for the 50 with the highest-dividend yields. Moreover, the high-dividend stocks suffered smaller drawdowns: -47% for all large-cap stocks compared with just 29% for the 50 highest yielding. Bear in mind that just because this (or any other) investment strategy has beaten the market over the very long term does not mean that the strategy will outperform in any particular year. In fact, it has historically been a toss-up whether the high-yielding stocks beat the overall large-cap market in a calendar year—about half the time the high-dividend stocks did better, but during the other half of the years the overall market did better.

The other conclusion we can draw from *What Works on Wall Street* is that a high yield is not always a good prognostic indicator. In addition to the results from large company stocks, O'Shaughnessy also reported a study that looked at the performance of the 50 highest-yielding stocks selected from publicly traded companies of any size, large or small. When he looked at their performance, it turned out that they did return a bit more than the overall market, but at *higher* risk. Taking both returns and risk into account, there was no advantage to the high-dividend yield strategy *unless* you restricted your consideration to large-company stocks.

A second set of studies comes from Wisdom Tree, which is a company that sponsors a number of ETFs generally based on the idea of overweighting stocks that are bargains relative to the overall market.[3] Wisdom Tree used a larger group of dividend-paying stocks (compared with the 50-stock portfolios that O'Shaughnessy generated). Also, instead of weighting each stock equally in their dividend strategy, Wisdom Tree weighted each stock according to the total dollar amount of dividends paid, calculated as dividend per share times the number of shares outstanding. Even though dividend yield is not explicitly used to calculate each stock's weight in the index, as a practical matter, an index weighted by the dollar amount of dividends paid will have a higher-dividend yield than traditional market indexes. For example, a dividend-weighted index of all U.S. stocks (The Wisdom Tree Dividend Index) yielded 3.7% as of May 2009, compared with a yield of 2.5% for the MSCI U.S. Broad Market Index.

Wisdom Tree reports that in its hypothetical study, which looked at data from 1964 to 2006, its dividend-weighted stock indexes returned more and had less risk compared with traditional benchmarks drawn from the same segments of the market. Unlike O'Shaughnessy, Wisdom Tree reported that a dividend-oriented strategy outperformed not only for large stocks, but also for all stocks, small-cap stocks, and mid-cap stocks as well. (I suspect that the discrepancy arose because O'Shaughnessy's hypothetical strategy of investing equally in stocks with the highest-dividend yields was more liable to invest in troubled small companies sporting high-dividend yields that were unsustainable.)

Neither of the dividend-oriented strategies mentioned previously would be practical for most individual investors who wanted to buy each individual stock for themselves. However, there are a number of ETFs that implement strategies designed to maximize dividend income. This is a big advantage because with an ETF you can get an entire portfolio of high-dividend stocks in just one transaction. ETFs would appear to be an ideal vehicle for this purpose because their below-average expense ratios leave more dividend income for the shareholders.

Table 11–1 lists selected dividend-oriented ETFs, as well as the Vanguard Total U.S. Market ETF (VTI) for comparison. The take-home message from Table 11–1 is that not all dividend-oriented ETFs are alike. Each one uses a different method to select the stocks in its portfolio. The result is that each dividend ETF can have varying exposures to different sectors of the markets and different dividend yields. Figure 11–1 shows an example of how during crucial periods, their performance can differ as well. The dividend yields shown in Table 11–1 are SEC yields (if available online) or the annualized yield based on the most recent quarterly dividend distribution. Getting information about the dividend yield on an ETF can be as tricky (or more so) as getting information about the yield to maturity of a bond fund. (See the sidebar "Know What Dividends You Will Really Be Getting from Your High-Dividend Investments.")

Wisdom Tree offers a dozen dividend-oriented ETFs in addition to the ones listed in Table 11–1, many of them fairly specialized (e.g., Japan Small-cap Dividend Fund). If you are curious, go to www.wisdomtree.com and click on the Dividend Analysis link. There is an excellent article that lists dividend-oriented ETFs from many different providers and contains links to their respective Web sites at Stock-Encyclopedia.com (http://etf.stock-encyclopedia.com/category/high-dividend-etfs.html).

Table 11-1   *Selected High-Dividend ETFs*

| Name | Ticker Symbol | Yield (December 2009) | Major Sectors and Other Comments |
|---|---|---|---|
| iShares Dow Jones U.S. Select Dividend Index ETF | DVY | 3.9% | Multi-cap U.S. equities; 23% utilities, 19% industrials, 12% financials |
| SPDR S&P Dividend ETF | SDY | 3.7% | 14% financials, 21% utilities, 16% industrials |
| Wisdom Tree Emerging Market Equity Income Fund | DEM | 4.6% | 25% materials, 17% financials, 14% telecomm and 11% technology; 50% mid-caps; the rest split evenly between large-caps and small-caps |
| Wisdom Tree Dividend ex-Financials | DTN | 4.3% | Evenly split between large- and mid-caps; largest sector weight is utilities (17%); and the ETF is spread among many different sectors |
| Wisdom Tree Equity Income Fund | DHS | 3.3% | 70% large-caps, 20% mid-caps, 10% small-caps 35% financials, 22% consumer staples, 7% utilities |
| Wisdom Tree Small-Cap Dividend Fund | DES | 4.1% | 43% financials, 16% consumer cyclical, just 4% utilities |
| Wisdom Tree Pacific-ex-Japan Equity Income Fund | DNH | 4.8% | 46% financials, 15% industrials, just 2% utilities Pretty evenly split among large-, mid-, and small-caps; mainly Australian companies |
| Vanguard U.S. Total Market ETF (broad-market, for comparison) | VTI | 2.4% | 19% technology, 16% financials, 4% utilities, 10%–13% each in health care, consumer staples, consumer discretionary, energy, and industrials |

## KNOW WHAT DIVIDENDS YOU WILL REALLY BE GETTING FROM YOUR HIGH-DIVIDEND INVESTMENTS

Reported yields for ETFs or even individual stocks can mislead you about the level of dividend income you will receive in the future. The problem arises when the reported yield is based on dividends paid in the preceding year that will not be maintained going forward.

One example is General Electric (GE). If you had looked up General Electric on http://moneycentral.msn.com in May 2009 you would have seen a reported dividend payout of $1.24, representing a yield of 9.5%. But the company announced a cut in its quarterly dividend from 31 cents a share to 10 cents a share on Feb. 27, 2009. Based on a share price of $13/share, the dividend yield going forward would be 40 cents/year divided by $13, or 3.1%, not the 9.5% reported based on past dividends.

For another example, we can look at the Wisdom Tree Web site, which reports both an SEC yield and a "net dividend yield" for its equity ETFs. The net dividend yield of an ETF reflects the dividend payouts received from the stocks in the ETF's portfolio during the past 12 months less foreign withholding taxes (if any) as a percentage of the current ETF share price. One of the Widsom Tree's ETFs, the Wisdom Tree Equity Income Fund (DHS), reported an eye-popping 7.5% dividend rate based on the May 2009 price of the ETF. But its SEC yield was just 4.1% at the time. The SEC yield is based only on dividends paid in the past month, and is, therefore, potentially more accurate in the face of recent dividend reductions.

From 2008 to 2009, many companies cut their dividends. For example, the total dividends paid by the companies in the S&P 500 Index dropped by 20% between May 2008 and May 2009. This is an unusually severe pace of dividend cuts. It is more common for companies to maintain or increase their dividends overall. In this environment, when evaluating dividend-paying equity ETFs, use the SEC yield, which reflects the stream of dividends during the most recent 30-day period. If you are evaluating individual stocks, you should search each company on Google to locate the most recent dividend announcement and use that information to calculate the prospective dividend yield. Remember, unlike the case with bonds, a company is not required to maintain its current level of dividend payouts in the future. But by doing a little homework, you can at least protect yourself from mistakenly assuming that last year's dividend stream will recur during the coming year.

You do have to be careful when you invest in a high-dividend equity portfolio because such portfolios are usually not representative of the broad stock market. Rather, they emphasize certain sectors that tend to pay above-average dividends, most notably utilities. Until 2009, financial stocks overall were big dividend payers and were therefore heavily represented in most high-dividend ETFs. Unfortunately for dividend investors, financial stocks bore the brunt of the 2007–2009 bear market. As a result, most ETFs whose goal is to maximize dividend income fared as badly or worse than the overall stock market during this period, notwithstanding the previous history of success with dividend-oriented strategies.

You can see this in Figure 11–1, which shows the total returns of the Vanguard Total Market ETF (VTI) as a benchmark, along with the performances (2006–2009) of three of the U.S. equity ETFs from Table 11–1. The SPDR S&P Dividend ETF (SDY) had a 55% drawdown in the most recent bear market, which is about the same as the worst loss suffered by the overall U.S. stock market. The other dividend-oriented ETFs in Figure 11–1 (iShares Dow Jones U.S. Select Dividend ETF, DVY, and the Wisdom Tree Dividend Index ETF, DHS) had drawdowns of 63% and 67%, respectively.

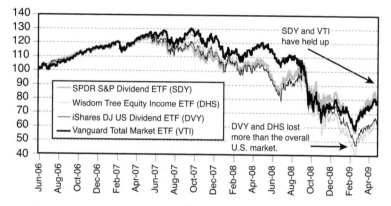

**Figure 11–1** *Total returns for selected dividend ETFs and broad U.S. market ETF, 2006–2009*

# Recommended Foreign Equity ETF: Wisdom Tree Emerging Markets Equity Income ETF (DEM)

This ETF appears to be an excellent vehicle for individual investors for a number of reasons. First, emerging markets generally appear to have the brightest investment prospects in the decades ahead. (Emerging markets are developing countries with significant stock markets, including China, Taiwan, Brazil, India, South Korea, and South Africa, to name the largest.) Second, in its real-time history since mid-2007 and in hypothetical history going back to 1996, the Wisdom Tree Emerging Markets Equity Income ETF (DEM) has outperformed iShares MSCI Emerging Market Index ETF (EEM), as shown in Figure 11–2. In fact, even though emerging market stocks are generally riskier than U.S. stocks, the drawdown of the Wisdom Tree Emerging Market Equity Income ETF (DEM) during the 2007–2009 bear market was 52%, which was no worse than the 55% drawdown of the U.S. market overall. In comparison, the broader-based iShares MSCI Emerging Markets Index ETF (EEM) had a worst drawdown of 66%. We saw in Figure 11–1 that previously safe dividend strategies for U.S. stocks were not safer than the broader stock market in 2007–2009. However, it is somewhat encouraging that the dividend-oriented strategy for the Emerging Markets Equity Income ETF (DEM) remained safer than the overall emerging market stock universe.

The reason why the Emerging Markets Equity Income ETF (DEM) held up relatively well compared with other dividend-oriented ETFs is that even before the bear market of 2007–2009, DEM was never as heavily weighted in financial stocks as were dividend-oriented ETFs that drew from developed-country stock markets. In the wake of that bear market, financial stocks are now less heavily weighted in many dividend-oriented ETFs.

There is no guarantee of future performance, but even if the Emerging Markets Equity Income ETF (DEM) simply matches the performance of broad emerging market ETFs in the future, it would still be a good way to diversify other elements of an equity portfolio and would be a good source of dividend income.

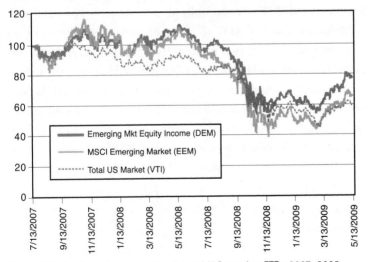

Figure 11–2    *Emerging market and total U.S. market ETFs, 2007–2009*

# Recommended Dividend Portfolio

The mix of sectors in the Wisdom Tree Emerging Market Equity Income ETF (DEM) has always been distinct from the mix of sectors in other dividend-oriented ETFs, and Table 11–1 shows that this remains the case. That observation raises the question of whether there could be a benefit from combining DEM with another dividend-oriented ETF so that the combination would have a better balance between risk and return than either ETF would by itself. The answer is yes, at least historically.

The dividend-ETF portfolio I recommend includes the two safest dividend-oriented ETFs: the SPDR S&P Dividend ETF (SDY) and the Wisdom Tree Emerging Market Equity Income ETF (DEM). Combinations of these two ETFs have been slightly safer than either ETF alone during the 2007–2009 bear market.

Normally, emerging market stocks are riskier than developed country stocks but the 2007–2009 bear market was anomalous in that the Emerging Market Equity Income ETF (DEM) lost less than U.S. dividend-oriented ETFs. If you utilized only the real-time data from 2007–2009 on DEM and SDY to calculate the safest high-dividend portfolio, you would find that a mix of two thirds in DEM and one third in SDY would produce the least drawdown. However, if you look further back in market history (using hypothetical data on DEM back to 1996), you would find that allocating 20% of your dividend-oriented equity ETFs to DEM would be more appropriate because from 1996 to 2007, DEM was indeed riskier than Wisdom Tree dividend indexes of developed-country stocks. This means that the remaining 80% of your equity would be from developed countries.

We saw in Chapter 10, "Why Even Conservative Investors Need Some Exposure to Other Markets," an income investor should have 25% of his or her investments in stocks. Of that 25%, I propose that

5% (one fifth of equity capital) should be in DEM and 10% (two fifths of equity capital) in SDY. The remaining 10% should be allocated to covered call writing, which we discuss in the next chapter.

There are two more points to mention about high-dividend ETFs. The first is to reemphasize that even though high-yielding stocks have traditionally been thought of as safer than the overall market, buying and holding a high-dividend portfolio has not by any means been nearly as safe as holding investment-grade bonds or using sell stops to manage the risks of high-yield bonds. Diversifying and selecting the safest of the dividend-paying investments does pay off, but even these measures are far from sufficient to protect you from stock market risk. It is for this reason that as a conservative investor, you need to limit yourself to 25% in equities. Even this modest level of exposure would have produced losses of almost 10% of your entire portfolio during 2008. You can increase your exposure above this level only if you can tolerate the risk of another 30%–40% drawdown in your equity holdings during a future bear market or if you employ additional risk-containment strategies for your equities (such as using technical analysis to tell you when to move from stocks to cash).

Second, the Wisdom Tree Emerging Market Equity Income ETF (DEM) is not heavily traded. The average daily volume for the three months ending 5/15/09 was just 50,000 shares/day, compared with over 300,000 shares/day for the SPDR S&P Dividend Index ETF (SDY) and over a million shares a day for the iShares Dow Jones Select U.S. Dividend Index ETF (DVY). The lack of activity in DEM makes it difficult for money managers to use, but should not be an obstacle to the individual investor if you use a trustworthy stockbroker. When you buy DEM for yourself, specify the share price you want to pay (based on the bid/ask quotes that your broker can give you). That is called a limit order, which you should place at the ask price if you want a speedy execution. Don't give a broker a market order (telling him to buy the shares immediately at whatever price he has to pay) with thinly traded ETFs unless your broker has a record of good execution for your account.

# Conclusion

A number of equity ETFs pay dividend yields of 4% per year or more, comparable with what you can get from investment-grade bonds. They also offer you the potential for capital gains and for the level of income they pay to increase over time. However, these ETFs have entailed significant price risks, as with any other stock market investment. Therefore, as a conservative investor, you should limit your equity exposure to 25% of your total long-term investments, no matter how safe you believe the stock market to be.

As an individual investor, you can put together a diversified high-dividend portfolio using just two ETFs: the SPDR S&P Dividend ETF (SDY) and the Wisdom Tree Emerging Market Equity Income ETF (DEM). An overall investment program that could produce 5% per year in ongoing investment income in addition to potential growth might consist of the following:

- 10% high-dividend U.S. stocks (SDY)
- 5% high-dividend emerging market stocks (DEM)
- 10% covered call writing (see Chapter 12)
- 10% preferred stocks (see Chapter 9)
- 25% high-yield bond funds (using a stop loss for risk control, see Chapter 7)
- 40% investment-grade bonds (selecting from the bond investments described in Chapters 4, 5, 6, and 8)

# chapter 12

# Using Options to Earn Income

If you have ever consulted a full-service stockbroker in search of a relatively conservative equity investment strategy, you might have heard about "covered call writing." This chapter explains how you can use ETF options to reduce your investment risk. However, even though covered call writing is widely touted as a conservative strategy, you will see here why that characterization is misleading. Covered call writing can have a place in your safe investment portfolio, but it is no panacea for stock market risk.

## What Are Stock Options?

A stock option (call option) is a legal agreement between two investors in which the call option buyer pays for the right (but not the obligation) to buy a stock from the call option seller at a predetermined price before the predetermined expiration date of the contract.

Let's see how this works with a simple example. Investor A thinks that the S&P 500 Index will be higher in a month from now, but is afraid of the possible losses if his outlook is wrong and, contrary to his expectations, the S&P 500 Index should happen to fall significantly. It turns out that there is a way for Investor A to buy insurance, so that if his prediction of a higher market comes true, he will reap the gains, but if the market falls, he will not be on the hook for more than he paid for the insurance. This type of insurance is known as a call option.

If you own a call option on a stock or ETF, you have the right but not the obligation to buy 100 shares of the stock at a predetermined price at any time before the expiration of your option. Let's see how this would work for Investor A, who wants to take a position that profits if the S&P 500 Index rises.

Investor A can act on his outlook by buying a call option on the S&P 500 SPDR (ticker SPY), an ETF that tracks the S&P 500 Index. (Roughly speaking, the value of one share of SPY is one tenth the level of the index, so if the S&P 500 Index is trading at 900, SPY will trade at approximately $90/share.) Suppose SPY is at $90/share and Investor A buys a call option that gives him the right (but not the obligation) to buy 100 shares of SPY at $90/share anytime within the next month. The price that the option buyer must pay to buy the shares if he so chooses is called the *strike price*, which, in this example, is $90. If SPY rises to $95 by the end of the month, the option that Investor A owns will allow him to buy 100 shares at $90 and resell them immediately on the open market at $95, for a profit of $5 per share, or $500 total. On the other hand, if SPY closes below $90/share at the end of the month, Investor A does nothing with his option, instead letting it expire. In this way, the option that Investor A purchased does not place him on the hook for any losses in SPY between the time he purchased his option and its expiration. However, the option does allow Investor A full participation in any profits that might be had in the event that SPY rises.

So far, this sounds good for Investor A. If Investor A buys investment insurance in the form of a call option, there must be someone to sell it to him. We will call the person at the other end of the insurance transaction "Investor B." If Investor B sells a call option to Investor A that gives Investor A the right (but not the obligation) to buy 100 SPY from him at $90/share within a month, Investor B will lose money if SPY finishes the month above $90 because he will have to purchase 100 shares of SPY at the market price above $90 and deliver them to

Investor A for only $90. On the other hand, if SPY finishes the month below $90, Investor B will not get the opportunity to sell at the strike price of $90/share. He will instead be left holding the stock. In short, Investor B who sold the call option forfeits gains in his stock if the market goes up, but has to eat all the losses if it goes down. Figure 12–1 shows the value of an option for SPY at $90/share at the time of its expiration. For every dollar per share by which SPY exceeds $90, the option is worth a dollar. However, the option can never be worth less than zero.

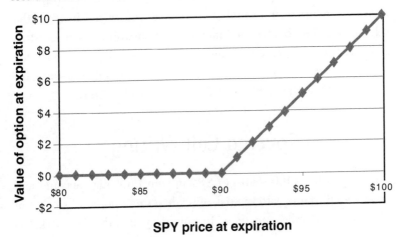

**Figure 12–1** *Value at expiration of a call option to buy SPY at $90*

This all sounds too good to be true for Investor A, who has no risk if the market falls but enjoys the full benefit of profits if the market rises. Investor B seems to be a sucker: He loses if the market rises, but makes nothing if it falls.

So why would Investor B agree to sell a call option to Investor A? Investor B will do so only if the amount of money that Investor A pays him is sufficient to cover the risk of loss. In other words, when Investor A buys a call option from Investor B, Investor A is really paying B to shoulder all the risk.

If SPY should happen to stay flat for the month, the call option for which A paid B will not be worth anything, like an insurance policy in the absence of any claim. So in that case, B made a profit while A turned a flat market into a loss.

Investors A and B do not need to know each other. There exist options exchanges where investors can go to buy or sell options from each other. The Options Clearing Corporation matches the payments and obligations between buyers and sellers of options, anonymously. If you buy or sell an option on an exchange, you do not get to specify precisely the price or expiration date that you want. Instead, the exchange has a predetermined menu of options from which investors can choose. It is the case for many stocks and less-popular ETFs that the available selection of options can be quite limited. But the most popular ETFs such as SPY offer a wide variety of options.

# Covered Call Writing

Suppose you have 100 shares of SPY in your brokerage account and you are comfortable with the risk of holding this amount of stock, but want some immediate income. In any given month, the market is almost as likely to go down as to rise, so waiting for a price change will not be reliable in the near term. Instead, you can sell a call option against your stock. Selling a call option against stock you already own is called covered call writing.

Returning to the preceding example, suppose that SPY is $90 and you sell a call option against your 100 shares for $300. The option you sell expires in a month and allows the owner of the option to buy your 100 shares from you at $90/share, regardless of the market price of your stock at that time. If SPY stays at $90 or falls lower during the month, you have collected $300 for doing nothing. In fact, if SPY falls from $90/share to $87/share, the $300 you collected cancels out the loss in your 100 shares of stock—writing the covered call turned a losing month for the market into a neutral month for you. If SPY falls from $90/share to $84/share, the $300 you collected will cancel half of the loss you would have taken if you had simply held onto your shares without selling any options. Because the effect of writing covered calls is to reduce the size of your losses compared with simply holding the shares without writing the calls, covered call writing is often (erroneously) viewed as a conservative strategy.

On the other hand, if your shares of SPY rise to $92, you would have to part with your shares for only $90 at the expiration of the option you sold, forfeiting a potential gain of $2/share (or $200 total for your 100 shares). But that is not so bad because you took in $300 for selling the option, which is more than the $200 you forfeited. It is only in the event that your shares rise further than the price you received for selling the option that you would regret selling the call.

From the perspective of safety, the problem with covered call writing is that you must bear nearly the full brunt of major market declines. For example, in October 2008, SPY lost some 15%, falling from $113 to $96—a loss of $17/share. Any amount of money that you would have collected for selling call options against SPY for the month of October would have been at best a small fraction of this loss. Months like October 2008 do not occur frequently, but it would take only a few hits like this to derail your financial plans. Note that when you set up a covered call position, you are not locked in for the full remaining life of the option. You can always close out your position by buying back the call you sold, and selling the shares you own. So if you establish a covered call position and you want to take profits or cut losses early, you can cut and run.

# Getting Income from Writing Covered Calls

There are two sources of potential income from covered call writing. The first and most important is the option premium you collect each month for writing the call. In the case of options against SPY, that can typically amount to 2% per month of the value of the underlying shares. The scarier the stock market landscape, the greater the amount of income you will take in by writing covered calls (and the greater the risk you bear in holding the underlying stock). The second (and smaller) source of investment income is the dividend yield of SPY itself, which was just 2.0% per year in late 2009.

If you write a covered call on the S&P 500 SPDR (SPY) for 2% of the value of the shares, you might psychologically be tempted to view this 2% (which you can collect each month) as money in the bank. Unfortunately, that is not the case. You will need most of the money you take in by selling options to maintain the value of your investment. If the investor to whom you sold your option decides to buy the shares from you at the strike price (which is known as "calling your shares") because the shares have risen above the strike price, you will have to buy your shares back at the higher price to repeat the strategy next month. On the other hand, if your stock loses money by options expiration, you will need some of the option premium you took in to offset that loss. So even though it might appear at first blush that you can take in 15%–20% per year (as a percentage of the underlying stock) in option premium, you would in practice deplete your investment fairly quickly if you spent all of that. Rather, I recommend that you plan to take 6% per year to spend out of the capital you allocate to writing covered calls against the S&P 500 SPDR (SPY). If the strategy returns more than that (which I would expect but cannot guarantee), the extra return will help your investment grow over time.

In that happy outcome, the disposable income that a 6% withdrawal rate provides would also grow over time to help you keep up with inflation.

# Let's Look at the Record

The Chicago Board Options Exchange (CBOE) maintains a historical record of how covered call writing has performed against a hypothetical stock portfolio that tracks the S&P 500 Index.[1] The top half of Figure 12–2 shows the total return of the S&P 500 Index from 1988 to 2009, along with the total return of a covered call writing strategy against the same index. The bottom part of the figure shows the value of a hypothetical investment in covered call writing on the S&P 500 Index divided by the total return of the S&P 500 itself. When this graph is rising, it means that covered call writing is performing better than the S&P 500 itself, as occurred from October 2007 to November 2008, 2000–2003, and 1989–1995, for example. (That is, it is either making more profit or losing less.) When the graph is falling, it means that the S&P 500 Index outperformed the covered call writing strategy, as occurred in 1995–1997. When the graph is flat, as it was from 1997–2000 and 2004–2006, it means that both strategies are generating similar returns. As a general rule, covered call writing is less profitable than simply buying an index investment during very strong market climates. During such periods, the average gains in the market exceed the average price you would receive from selling calls against the stock you owned. Conversely, during periods of flat or falling markets, covered call writing outperforms an investment in the index alone.

You can see that over the entire 1988–2009 period, covered call writing has been slightly more profitable and slightly less risky than the S&P 500 Index itself. These results certainly speak well of the strategy. (Past results do not guarantee the future performance of any investment.) However, the results of covered call writing can hardly be called safe because a covered call writer would have lost more than one third of his investment during the 2000–2003 bear market and more than 40% during the 2007–2009 bear market. Still, at the low points of these two bear markets, investors in just the S&P 500 Index would have lost 47% and 55%, respectively—significantly worse losses than experienced by the covered call writing strategy.

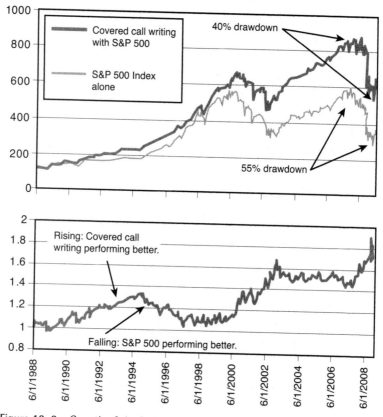

**Figure 12–2**  *Growth of the S&P 500 Index and of writing covered calls against this index, 1988–2009*

# How to Implement a Covered Call Writing Strategy

The easiest way to undertake a program of covered call writing against the basket of stocks in the S&P 500 Index is to avail yourself of an ETF that implements this strategy: the PowerShares S&P 500 Buy-Write ETF, ticker symbol PBP. From the time of its inception in late 2007 through mid-2009, PBP has mostly tracked the theoretical performance of the strategy very well. There were two glitches on two different dates in 2008 when for some reason the ETF closing prices deviated by several percent from the benchmark. You need to watch out for this sort of event in ETFs or stocks that do not trade very actively. Before making any transactions in PBP, make sure that its price change from the closing price the day before is consistent with the price change in the S&P 500 Index from the day before. (Because covered call writing reduces volatility, the price change in PBP should be smaller than the change in the S&P 500 Index.) If there is a discrepancy, be wary about placing any trading orders.

There are three costs of using the PowerShares S&P 500 Buy-Write ETF: the ETF expense ratio, the trading costs that the ETF itself incurs, and the bid-ask spread. The expense ratio of the PowerShares ETF (PBP) is 0.75% per year, which is high compared with most ETFs that I like to use but which is still tolerable. As the result of this expense ratio and the ETF's own trading expenses, PBP has lagged the theoretical performance of the strategy by 1.5% per year.

You will also have to contend with the bid-ask spread when you buy or sell shares of PBP through your stockbroker. The PowerShares S&P 500 Buy-Write ETF is not heavily traded, so transacting 500 shares (approximately $9,000) could cost you 1/4%–1/2%, depending on market conditions at the time you buy. This trading cost represents a major burden, so you should only buy PBP if you intend to make at least a yearlong commitment to the covered call writing strategy.

If you have the expertise, an alternative to investing in the PowerShares S&P 500 Buy-Write ETF is to buy individual ETF shares and write covered calls in your own brokerage account. Specifically, you would buy shares of the S&P 500 SPDR (SPY). For every 100 shares of SPY you purchase, you would sell one call option. There are many call options against SPY. To select the correct one, you need to look for the strike price and the expiration date that you want.

Recall that the strike price is the amount that the option owner must pay to buy the stock if he chooses to. If you write a covered call, the strike price is the amount you will get for your shares if they reach or exceed the strike price. However, if your shares trade below the strike price, nobody will buy them from you at the strike price. So if you write a covered call, the strike price represents a ceiling on how much you can possibly get for your stock.

The expiration date of an option is the last date that the owner of a call option can exercise his right to buy the stock. All else being equal, the more time that remains until the expiration date, the more expensive an option costs because there is more opportunity for the stock to rise above the strike price. There is one options expiration date each month, on the third Friday.

*To implement a covered call writing strategy against the basket of stocks in the S&P 500 Index, you would write the SPY call with the nearest expiration date whose strike price is closest to (but not below) the current price of the shares of SPY.*

Let's see how that would work with an example: At some point when the stock market was open during the day on May 27, 2009, the S&P 500 SPDR (SPY) was trading at $90.43. The nearest expiration date was June 19, 2009, and the nearest available strike price was $91.

To initiate a covered call writing strategy, for every 100 shares of SPY, you would write a June 91 call, which (as of this writing) would have brought in $2.12 in option premium.

The bid-ask spread in trading SPY and its options is usually negligible, but brokerage commissions might be significant. Recall that the total cost of executing this strategy with the PowerShares ETF (PBP) is projected at 2% for the first year: 1.5% deviation from the theoretical benchmark and 0.5% in bid-ask spread. For doing it yourself (with SPY and its options) to be more economical, your trading costs would have to be less than 2% per year, or 0.17% per month. One hundred shares of SPY represent an investment of approximately $9,000, and 0.17% of this is approximately $15. This means that if you can execute the covered call strategy at a cost of less than $15 per 100 shares of SPY, you could be better off than if you bought and held PBP for a year.

Many discount brokers charge a minimum commission of around $10 per transaction, so if you had just 100 shares of SPY to buy and one call to write (total of two transactions), your total commissions would amount to $20, more than 0.2% of the cost of the underlying 100 shares of SPY, which is more expensive than the costs entailed in owning the PowerShares ETF (PBP). On the other hand, if you are investing enough to buy 200 shares of SPY (total of $18,000) and sell two covered calls each month, your total transaction cost will still be $20, but because you are transacting in 200-share lots of SPY, your monthly commission costs would be just 0.1% (approximately) of the capital required to buy the underlying 200 shares of SPY. If you have the time and the inclination, buying SPY and writing calls in your own account would be potentially cheaper than owning the PowerShares ETF (PBP).

The implication is that investors with $10,000 or less to invest will almost certainly be better off buying and holding the PowerShares

S&P 500 Buy-Write ETF (PBP) than attempting to set up their own covered call strategy with SPY and its options. On the other hand, if you are adept at using a discount broker, have secured reasonable commission rates, and if you have more than $20,000 to invest (allowing you to transact 200-share lots of SPY), doing it yourself will probably be cheaper.

# Covered Call Writing against Indexes besides the S&P 500

The CBOE also maintains a hypothetical index of writing covered calls against the stocks in the Dow Jones Industrial Average, which, like the S&P 500 Index, represents large U.S. company stocks. You can compare the results on the CBOE Web site for this strategy with the results of buying and holding the ETF, which tracks the Dow Jones Industrial Average (called "Diamonds," ticker symbol DIA). From 1998 to 2009, DIA returned just 2.7% per year with a 52% drawdown. Covered call writing against the stocks of the Dow Jones Industrial Average would have returned 3.7% per year with a 36% drawdown during the same period. It goes without saying that if you expect stocks to fare as poorly in the future as they did from 1998 to 2009, you should not bother with any equity strategy at all. On the other hand, if you expect (as I do) that stocks will improve, returning potentially 8% per year or more in the decades ahead, you should find it encouraging that a covered call writing strategy against the stocks in the Dow Jones Industrial Average reduced risk by almost one third (from 52% to 36% drawdown).

You should not assume that every covered call writing strategy will match what happens with the S&P 500 Index, a basket of large, U.S. companies. For example, the CBOE also maintains an index

(BXR) that represents a strategy of buying the basket U.S. small company stocks in the Russell 2000 Index and selling covered calls against this index. Figure 12–3 shows the total returns from the Russell 2000 Index alone and from a covered call writing strategy using the Russell 2000 over an eight year period (2001–2009). As with the S&P 500 Index, covered call writing against the Russell 2000 Index during the period shown slightly outperformed the index itself. During this period, the worst loss in the index was 59% (similar to the 55% that the S&P 500 lost at its worst point). However, writing covered calls would have resulted in only a small decrease in this worst loss, from 59% to 53%. Recall that the degree of risk reduction writing covered calls against the S&P 500 Index was greater, from 55% to 40%. The implication is that the degree of safety you achieve with covered calls depends on the underlying investment. Covered call writing strategies have not produced the same degree of risk reduction for every index as they have for the S&P 500 Index or the Dow Jones Industrial Average.

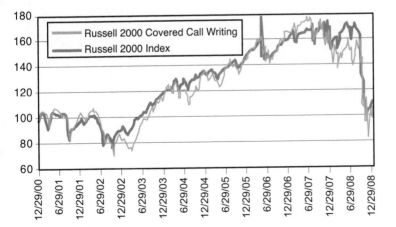

**Figure 12–3** *Growth of investments in the Russell 2000 Index and in covered call writing against that index, 2001–2009*

165

# Conclusion

Covered call writing can produce decent profits during months when the market is flat or rising, and can reduce losses during months when the market falls by a historically normal amount. When both risks and returns are taken into account, covered call writing has outperformed the S&P 500 Index during the 1986–2009 period—a strong record that speaks well of the strategy for this particular group of stocks. Unfortunately, covered call writing cannot completely protect you from the risks of a major market decline. Historically, covered call writing against the S&P 500 Index would have reduced bear market losses by more than one quarter, which is significant but not sufficient to constitute a complete program of investment safety.

# chapter 13

# Conclusion— Assembling the Program for Lifetime Investment Income

In this book, we have covered a number of different income-producing strategies that utilize a variety of bond and stock investments. Table 13–1 summarizes these strategies, their historical risks, and my projections for future returns in the coming decade (2010–2020). The strategies are listed from safest to riskiest. No future performance can be guaranteed, but these potential returns based on current interest rates are more likely to be realized than past returns from bonds when interest rates were far higher than they are now. Just to be on the safe side, I have anticipated equity returns of 8% per year for all the equity strategies, which is less than the 10% long-term historical annual return from the American stock market. In this final chapter, we discuss how you should put these strategies together to build an investment program for lifetime income.

Table 13-1    *Summary of Income-Producing Investment Strategies*

| Strategy | Projected Annual Return | Historical Drawdown |
|---|---|---|
| Treasury bills, money market funds, bank CDs | 0%–2% | None |
| Bond ladder with investment-grade bonds held until maturity | 3% | 0%–1% |
| Individual ten-year investment-grade bonds held until maturity | 4% | 0%–1% |
| Investment-grade total bond market index or recommended investment-grade bond mutual fund | 4% | -13% |
| High-yield bond funds (with stop loss) | 7% | -10% |
| Preferred stocks in nonfinancial companies | 6% | -20% to -25% |
| Covered call writing against S&P 500 SPDR (SPY) | 8% | -40% |
| High-dividend equity ETFs | 8% | -52% to -55% |

The safest strategies in Table 13–1, money market funds and bond ladders, also have the lowest current returns. The reason is that the levels of interest income from both depend in whole (money market funds) or in part (bond ladders) on short-term interest rates, which the Federal Reserve has set at close to zero to stimulate a recovery from the 2008–2009 recession. However, I am optimistic that these safest of investment strategies will become more profitable in the future. When the recovery does get under way, the Federal Reserve will likely boost rates significantly as it has in the past. (The most recent example: By 2003, the Fed lowered its short-term rate target, the Fed Funds Rate, to 1%. When the economy resumed growing at a brisk rate, the Fed hiked rates all the way up to 5.25% by 2006. Treasury bill and money market fund returns closely track the Fed Funds rate.) Eventual Federal Reserve rate hikes will again improve the returns available from short-term bond investments.

It would be nice to be able to recommend a single recipe for life-time income that would work for everyone, but in the current low-yield world, that is impossible. Instead, you must make a trade-off between potential returns and potential risks. Only you can decide how much risk you can tolerate or how much interest income you require, both emotionally and financially. Once you have decided how much risk to assume, you can select from among the several suggested investment programs that follow.

# For the Most Conservative Investor—A Program of Predictable Returns with Individual Bonds

If you cannot bear to watch market fluctuations, and desire strongly to know exactly what your returns will be, you need to stick with indi-vidual bonds in very solid companies or government entities and hold those bonds until they mature. At the level of interest rates prevailing as of late 2009, such a program should return approximately 4% per year if you buy 10-year taxable corporate bonds or 20-year municipal bonds.

Note that 4% per year is barely enough to keep up with inflation which means that if you adopt this approach, the purchasing power of your investments will probably erode over time if you spend even a modest fraction of your principal each year. The risk of depleting your principal or purchasing power makes this superconservative approach suitable mainly for investors who do not expect to live for more than 15 years, or who need at most 1%–2% per year of their principal to meet expenses.

In 2009, inflation was not a problem. However, the record level of federal budget deficits and the weakening of the U.S. dollar could change that in the years to come. As a result, I recommend that the investor looking for dependable returns during the coming decade or beyond should utilize the bond-ladder strategy that was described in Chapter 4, "Bond Ladders—Higher Interest Income with Less Risk." With a bond ladder, if interest rates rise down the road (as I expect they will at some point after 2010), you will at least be in a position to increase the level of income you derive from your investments.

The other option for the risk-averse investor who is also concerned about future inflation is to buy ten-year Treasury Inflation-Protected Securities (TIPS) and hold them until maturity, as discussed in Chapter 6, "The Safest Investment There Is—Treasury Inflation-Protected Securities (TIPS)." In October 2009, ten-year TIPS paid approximately 1.4%–1.5% per year plus inflation. If inflation returns to its historically typical level of 3%–4% per year, TIPS could well turn out to return more than ten-year investment-grade corporate bonds without any of the credit risk. To avoid the risk of owing more in taxes than you receive in coupon interest during a period of high inflation, you need to hold individual TIPS in a tax-deferred account such as an IRA.

If you are unable to purchase individual bonds, the investment-grade bond mutual funds discussed in Chapter 5, "Bond Mutual Funds—Where the Best Places Are for Your One-Stop Shopping," can offer many advantages to you, especially if you have less than $20,000 to invest or if you need access to your capital on short notice. However, unlike individual bonds, there is no holding period over which a fund is certain to generate a positive return. Also, be aware that investment-grade bonds suffered far greater risks in the 1970s than at any time since because of the extreme volatility in interest rates and inflation back then, before most existing bond mutual funds were established. For example, from 1979 to 1980, the Barclays Total U.S. Bond Market Index lost 13% (including interest) at its worst extent. It is not a foregone conclusion that such bad times will return to the bond market, nor is there any guarantee that they won't.

Because it is inevitable that you are assuming some risk when you buy a bond mutual fund, as a bond fund investor, you should probably incorporate some stock market exposure as well, for the reasons discussed in the following sections.

# For the Investor Who Needs to Spend a Little More and Is Willing to Take Some Risk to Do So—Allocate 25% of Your Portfolio to Stocks

The ten-year period from 1/1/2000 to 12/31/2009 was the worst decade for stocks since the 1930s. Although there are no guarantees, it has been the case historically that bad decades for stocks (such as the 1930s and 1970s) have been followed by stronger periods. Assuming (as I do) that the pendulum has already begun to swing back toward favoring stocks as an investment, conservative investors for whom present interest rates are too low to meet their needs should invest up to 25% of their portfolio in equities (with the remainder in investment-grade bonds and/or bond mutual funds).

Recall from Chapter 10, "Why Even Conservative Investors Need Some Exposure to Other Markets," that moving 25% of a hypothetical bond index portfolio into stocks did not increase the risk compared with holding only the bond index. In both cases, the worst historical drawdowns from 1976 to 2009 were in the 12%–13% range. But adding stocks did increase returns compared with holding just a bond index investment, and with interest rates now so low by historical standards, the potential profit advantage of holding some stocks could be even greater in the years ahead than in the past. I project that investment-grade bonds will return 4% per year and equities will return 8% per year, on average. That means that adding 25% stocks to an otherwise all-bond portfolio could boost your returns from 4% to 5% per year without significantly increasing your risk, compared with holding a bond index fund alone.

The equity investments with which I recommend you diversify a bond portfolio include either the high-dividend ETF program from Chapter 11, "Equity ETFs for Dividend Income," and the covered call writing strategy from Chapter 12, "Using Options to Earn Income," or a selection of two stock market index funds (S&P 500 and emerging markets). One of the high-dividend ETFs from Chapter 11 has the advantage of including exposure to developing countries (where future returns are expected to be greater than in developed country stocks). If current dividend income is not a concern, the simplest way to obtain equity exposure is to place 20% of your portfolio in an S&P 500 Index fund (such as the Vanguard 500 Index Fund, symbol VFINX) and 5% in an emerging market investment (such as Vanguard's Emerging Stock Market ETF, ticker symbol VWO). If you are able to implement a covered call writing strategy using the S&P 500 SPDR (SPY), as discussed in Chapter 12, you could reduce the risk of your equity investments with no loss of long-term profitability (assuming historical patterns repeat themselves).

# For the Investor Willing to Assume Some Risk and to Monitor His Portfolio— Allocate 25% of Your Capital to High-Yield Bond Fund Trading

A review of the different strategies listed in Table 13–1 reveals that high-yield bond funds appear to offer the best balance between risk and reward for the investor willing to assume the 10% historical drawdown risk. The only other strategies in Table 13–1 that can potentially match the returns of high-yield bond fund trading are equity strategies. But equity strategies have had several times the risk for relatively small added return compared with high-yield bond funds.

The reason not to place all your capital into high-yield bond funds is that the future remains uncertain. 2008 saw unprecedented losses in high-yield bond funds, frequently in excess of 40% at their worst point (but not for investors who used stop losses successfully). Although it appears that the financial markets are out of the woods as of late 2009, it would be unwise to put all your eggs into the high-yield basket after the unexpected explosion of risk we saw in 2008. I must repeat the warning that buying and holding high-yield bond funds on a continuous basis through thick and thin has proven to be too risky and not rewarding enough to be worth your while. High-yield bond funds belong in your portfolio only if you are comfortable implementing the sell-stop risk-management strategy of Chapter 7, "High-Yield Bond Funds—Earn the Best Yields Available while Managing the Risks," either on your own or with the help of an investment advisor.

Even if you are not concerned about a repeat of 2008, there is one other disadvantage of high-yield bond fund trading: It does not produce steady income the way a portfolio of investment-grade bonds does. There have been prolonged periods (such as occurred much of the time from 1999 to 2002) when conditions in the high-yield market were unfavorable, and returns were close to zero. If such a period occurs again, you would have to dip into principal to meet your expenses during that time. Dipping into principal on occasion is no tragedy in the context of a long-term successful investment program, but a safety-conscious investor might find it too stressful.

If high-yield bond fund trading appeals to you, start with 25% of your portfolio in high yields. Up to 25% can be in equities, leaving 50% for investment-grade bonds. This investment mix could potentially return 6% per year—three-quarters of what you might earn from the stock market with perhaps a quarter of the risk. If you are concerned about keeping up with inflation while meeting your expenses over the next 15 years or more, this is the portfolio I recommend.

# Preferred Stocks—Boost Your Interest Income with Less Effort

Table 13–1 shows that the balance between risk and reward for preferred stocks has been inferior to that of high-yield bond fund trading, which is due to the absence of a proven risk-management strategy for preferred stocks. However, preferred stocks might belong in your portfolio anyway. If you are unwilling or unable to implement a sell-stop strategy for high-yield bond funds, you could instead place up to 10% of your capital into the sort of preferred stocks I recommended in Chapter 9, "Preferred Stocks—Obtain Higher Yields Than You Can with Corporate Bonds." In that case, your portfolio would consist of 65% in investment-grade bonds, 25% in equities, and 10% in preferred stocks and would not require ongoing monitoring by you except to initially select the preferred stocks to purchase and to replace any that are called.

As an investment manager, I find preferred stocks attractive as a substitute for investment-grade bonds *to a limited extent* because of the difference in yields. However, placing more than 50% of a client's portfolio outside of investment-grade bonds or bond funds requires watching the market and the portfolio closely, and utilizing additional risk-management tools that are beyond the scope of this book.

# Conclusion

For most of the 1980s and 1990s, the safety-conscious investor was able to secure an attractive level of interest income at low risk with a straightforward portfolio of investment-grade bonds. Even as recently as mid-2007, bank CDs offered 5% per year, risk free. Unfortunately, today's investor in search of income has a much tougher challenge because interest rates are at record lows. My goal in writing this book has been to give you the techniques and insights you need to wrest higher levels of ongoing income from a relatively barren environment without exposing yourself to excessive risk. I hope that what you have learned will bring you greater success in your income investing.

# Endnotes

## Chapter 1

1. http://www.brainyquote.com/quotes/authors/y/yogi_berra.html

## Chapter 2

1. Technically, Treasury *bonds* is the name applied to Treasury borrowing for periods exceeding ten years, whereas borrowings for one to ten years are called Treasury *notes*. The Barclays Capital U.S. Treasury Total Return Index listed in Table 2–1 includes all outstanding Treasury notes and bonds.

2. Source: Mutual Fund Expert database, 2/28/2009.

3. National municipal bond fund average from Mutual Fund Expert database, 2/28/2009. This data covers 11/30/1976–2/28/2009, which is a shorter period than the other indexes listed in the table.

4. Source of yield data: http://www.federalreserve.gov, Federal Reserve release H.15, "Selected Interest Rates," historical data. The yield in the table for Treasury bonds is the average of one-year and ten-year yields from the Federal Reserve Web site. The yield in the table for corporate bonds represents the average of Aaa and Baa yields reported on the Federal Reserve Web site.

5. Bond Buyer Index of yields on general obligation municipal bonds maturing in 20 years, accessed in Federal Reserve Release H-15, Historical Data, http://www.federalreserve.gov.

6. For the purposes of this example, we assume that bond interest is paid to you continuously during the period you own a bond, rather than in lump sums once every six months. As a practical matter, you do, in fact, receive interest for just the time you own the bonds, as explained in the later section "Buying Bonds Far from Coupon Payment Dates."

7. To clarify the use of the words *broker* and *dealer*, a *broker* is a company who holds the assets in your account, deposits coupon payments in your account for bonds you hold, takes your bond order, and, if the transaction is completed, delivers the bonds you purchased to your account and delivers the cash to pay for the purchase from your account to whoever sold you the bonds. A *dealer* is a firm that actually buys bonds to hold in their own inventory, waiting to sell them to investors like yourself. Some brokers also function as dealers. Two such firms with whom I have had personal bond-buying experience are Morgan-Keegan and Smith Barney. Other brokers such as Schwab and T.D. Ameritrade do not maintain inventories of bonds for potential customers. Rather, they act only as a middleman for bond dealers.

# Chapter 3

1. Varma, Praveen. "Determinants of Recovery Rates on Defaulted Bonds and Loans for North American Corporate Issuers: 1983–2003." Moody's Credit Research. http://www.moodys.com/cust/content/content.ashx?source=S taticContent/Free%20pages/Credit%20Policy%20Research/ documents/current/2003000000444168.pdf accessed on 3/28/2009.

2. The stated percentages of outstanding U.S. corporate bonds at each rating level were obtained from Fitch Ratings (http://www.fitchratings.com), "U.S. Corporate Bond Market: A Review of Fourth-Quarter and 2008 Rating and Issuance Activity."

3. Moody's Investor Service, "Historical Default Rates of Corporate Bond Issuers, 1920–1999", January 2000, http://www.moodyskmv.com/research/whitepaper/52453.pdf accessed on 3/28/09. The data in Table 3–1 are taken from Exhibit 30 in the Moody's research report.

4. Ibid, exhibit 32.

5. Fitch Ratings (http://www.fitchratings.com), "U.S. Corporate Bond Market: A Review of Fourth-Quarter and 2008 Rating and Issuance Activity."

6. See, for example, the data on http://www.markit.com regarding its ABX Indices, which track the market value of a basket of asset-backed bonds.

7. *Systems and Forecasts.* Marvin Appel, editor. January 28, 2009. (http://www.systemsandforecasts.com)

# Chapter 4

1. There are more numerous target retirement date funds that contain different mixes of stocks and bonds, with the mix moving more heavily toward bonds as the target date approaches. Don't try to ladder this type of target-date fund because you will not achieve the desired results.

# Chapter 5

1. Mendez, Ignacio, and Jordan Werblow. "Taxation of Bond Discounts and Premiums." *The Tax Advisor* (August 1, 2000). http://www.allbusiness.com/personal-finance/individual-taxes/608680-1.html (accessed 3/31/09).

2. http://www2.goldmansachs.com/gsam/docs/fundsinst/performance/quarterly_performance/inst_shortdurationgovernmentfund_600002_20081231_fc.pdf (accessed 5/4/09).

3. This index was formerly known as the Lehman Brothers U.S. Aggregate Bond Index, but after going bankrupt in 2008, Lehman Brothers sold its indexing business to Barclays.

4. The figures of 70%–93% represent the ranking of the one-, three-, five-, or ten-year Sharpe ratio of VBMFX versus the same Sharpe ratios of all fixed-income funds in the 2/28/2009 edition of the Mutual Fund Expert database.

5. http://www.vanguard.com (accessed 10/3/09).

6. http://www.sitfunds.com/funds/government-performance.xml (accessed 11/23/09).

# Chapter 6

1. Specifically, the Consumer Price Index for Urban Consumers (called CPI-U) and calculated by the Bureau of Labor Statistics (part of the Department of Labor). Also, because CPI data are available only weeks after the fact, TIPS prices adjust according to the level of the CPI from two months earlier. For example, the change in TIPS principal value during April 2009 reflected the change in CPI-U during February 2009. CPI-U data are calculated only once each month. The Treasury interpolates month-to-month CPI data to obtain principal values for TIPS during the other days of the month.

2. Source: Federal Reserve Statistical Release H-15, historical data.

3. It might be easier to access this site by doing a Google search for "TIPS yields" or for "daily Treasury real yield curve" (as I did on 4/13/09) than by copying the entire URL.

# Chapter 7

1. Source: Mutual Fund Expert database, 3/31/2009.

2. See Chapter 8 in *Beating the Market Three Months at a Time* by Gerald and Marvin Appel (FT Press, 2008) for a quarterly approach.

# Chapter 8

1. Levitt, Arthur. "Muni Bonds Need Better Oversight: We Seem to Have a Major Debacle Every Decade." *Wall Street Journal* (op-ed page), May 9, 2009.

2. http://www.nuveen.com (accessed 10/03/09).

3. See "CDFA Spotlight: Default Risks of Conduit Bonds" by Stan Provus for an excellent summary of the Fitch studies from 1999, 2003, and 2007 (http://www.cdfa.net/cdfa/cdfaweb.nsf/pages/spotlightde-faultconduit.html, accessed 5/27/09).

4. Litvack, David, Abruzzo, Thomas, and Koo, Mia. "Special Report: Default Risk and Recovery Rates on U.S. Municipal Bonds." Fitch Ratings, 1/9/2007, http://www.fitchratings.com.

5. Source: http://www.munibondadvisor.com/BondInsurance.htm (accessed 4/28/09).

# Chapter 11

1. *Ibbotson SBBI 2008 Classic Yearbook*, Morningstar Inc., Chicago, 2008.

2. Finding the dividend yield on an index is not as straightforward as finding the yield on an individual stock. The dividend yield on the S&P 500 Index is reported weekly in the "Market Laboratory" section of *Barron's*, a financial newspaper. You can also infer the same information online by visiting http://www.spdrs.com and entering the ticker symbol SPY where indicated. SPY is the symbol for the S&P 500 SPDR, the first and one of the most popular ETFs, which tracks the S&P 500 Index. The fact sheet that you will find on this Web site reports its dividend yield.

3. Jeremy Siegel, Jeremy Schwartz, and Luciano Siracusano III. "The Unique Risk and Return Characteristics of Dividend-Weighted Stock Indexes." Wisdom Tree Investments Inc., 2007 (Wisdom Tree White Papers).

# Chapter 12

1. Historical data on this index, ticker symbol BXM, is available at the CBOE Web site: http://www.cboe.com/micro/bxm.

# Index

## A

above par, 19

Alpine Ultra Short Tax Optimized Income Fund (ATOIX), 98-99

American Century Tax-Free Bond Fund (TWTIX), 96

AMT (alternative minimum tax), municipal bonds and, 15

asset-backed bonds, 41-43

AT&T preferred stock, price risk, 117

auction rate preferred stocks, 130-131

## B

back-end sales charges, 54

bank loans, asset-backed bonds, 41-43

Barclays Capital U.S. Aggregate Bond Index, 59-60

below par, 19

Berra, Yogi, 3

bond insurance, 107-110

bond laddering, 45-49

bond market, 2

bond mutual funds

in bonds-only investment strategy, 170

diversification, 52-53

exchange-traded funds (ETFs), 64-65

expense ratio, 53

maturity date, lack of, 56

recommendations

*FPA New Income (FPNIX)*, 62

*Pimco Total Return Fund (PTTRX)*, 61-62

*SIT U.S. Government Security (SNGVX)*, 62

*Vanguard Total Bond Market Index Fund (VBMFX)*, 59-60

redemption fees, 55

sales loads, 54-55

SEC yield, 58-59

transaction costs, 51-52, 55

yield to maturity, determining, 56-58

# S

# Notes

# Notes

# Notes

# Notes

# Notes

# Notes

# Notes

# Notes

# Notes

# Notes

FT Press
FINANCIAL TIMES

In an increasingly competitive world, it is quality
of thinking that gives an edge—an idea that opens new
doors, a technique that solves a problem, or an insight
that simply helps make sense of it all.

We work with leading authors in the various arenas
of business and finance to bring cutting-edge thinking
and best-learning practices to a global market.

It is our goal to create world-class print publications
and electronic products that give readers
knowledge and understanding that can then be
applied, whether studying or at work.

To find out more about our business
products, you can visit us at www.ftpress.com.